6-20-80

THE PAPER ARISTOCRACY

by

Howard S. Katz

Books In Focus, Inc.
New York

Manufactured in the United States of America
First Printing

Library of Congress Catalog Card Number 76-467
ISBN 0-916728-00-5 Paperback Edition
ISBN 0-916728-01-3 Cloth Edition

Typography: A & Q Computer Typesetters
                    Royal Composing Room
Cover Illustration: Jack Goldsmith

To Alana, Temah and Mya

CONTENTS

ILLUSTRATIONS

ACKNOWLEDGEMENTS

I wish to extend my personal thanks to Don B. Duncan and Steve Zarlenga, without whose backing this book would not have been possible. Thanks also to Rana Arons as editor, Dolores Grande as indexer and Don Hauptman as idea man.

Further acknowledgement is due to:

Macmillan Publishing Co., Inc. for permission to quote from *The Revolutionary Generation* by E.B. Greene, © 1943.

Yale U. Press for permission to quote from *The Fathers of the Constitution* by Max Farrand, © 1921.

Peter Smith Publishers for permission to quote from *The Foundations of American Constitutionalism* by Andrew C. McLaughlin, © 1932.

Van Nostrand Reinhold Co. for permission to quote from *Economics and the Public Welfare* by Benjamin Anderson, © 1949.

The Academy of Political Science for permission to quote from *Political Science Quarterly,* © 1935.

New York Times Co. for permission to quote from "Economics 1—The Summit" in *New York Times Magazine,* Sept. 22, 1974 by Leonard Silk, © 1974.

Harcourt Brace Jovanovich, Inc. for permission to quote from *General Theory of Employment, Interest and Money* by John Maynard Keynes, © 1936.

Holt, Rinehart and Winston, Inc. for permission to quote from *A History of American Currency* by William G. Sumner, © 1874.

Author's Note:

Nothing in this book should be construed as being against the rich for being rich. I believe it is perfectly in accord with justice when a man gets rich by creating economic values, and it is quite legitimate when a man acquires wealth by a voluntary gift. What I am against are people who get rich by the use of force and fraud, who make themselves better off by making others worse off. The exposure of such a fraud and the spotlighting of the manner in which force is used for this end are the purposes of this book.

INTRODUCTION

This is a book about money concepts that matter! Only a handful of people around the world realize that, if a money system is "fair," it enables society to function with ease, with safety, with relative prosperity, with a low crime rate, with a low divorce rate, with less immorality in politics and more.

And if a money system is *unfair*, the reverse takes place, and we get Watergates and soaring crime and divorce. Money creates attitudes of good or bad, strong or weak morality through its soundness.

It's not necessary that I agree with every thought that author Howard Katz has written herein. Indeed all those who write introductions to books will surely feel the same—that in some cases they may even disagree violently here and there. But, especially in economics, which is a non-science, there is room for differing opinion even among those who basically stand together.

And I do stand together with Howard Katz, whose grasp of money is remarkable and his courage admirable. He's a "patriot" in the best sense, not for a flag (I don't think) but for his fellow man. He wants them to get a fair shake.

It's a crime of the highest order that the cause for sound money has been taken over by the wrong crowd. Or, the other way to say it is that the people who have most to gain from such things as gold backing and convertible currency and disciplinary money systems are the ones who fight it or ignore and consider it trivial or old fashioned. Those who have least to gain from it (relatively) are the biggest boosters of such fundamentals. It used to be the other way round, back in the days of the U.S. as a young country. Politics got it twisted.

But that is quibbling, because we all need, really need, a fair money system and sound money. And Howard Katz has made a valuable contribution here to a better understanding of not only the need but the solution possible.

I think you'll find his journey into inner space (your mind, if it's working properly) an interesting one. His conceptualizations are often unique and always imaginative and educational.

If we spread greater understanding of money we stand a better chance of a safe society.

> Harry D. Schultz, Ph.D., D.Sc.
> Lausanne-Amsterdam-London-Dusseldorf-Toronto

FOREWORD

THE DISMAL SCIENCE

Economics, dear reader, is one of the most important aspects of your life. You either work or are dependent for your life on someone who does work. Unless you are a rather odd recluse, you use money and engage in trade. And you probably spend a good part of your waking hours engaged in economic activity.

However, economics has become known as the Dismal Science—a title it acquired by virtue of being so boring. The reason the subject of economics is regarded as dismal is that economists have taken a false approach, which I call the *little brother complex*. Economists look upon the physical sciences (especially mathematics and physics) with the awe and admiration reserved for a little boy's attitude toward his older brother. They adopt a pseudo-scientific guise and try to imitate the physical sciences in every detail.

Economics is a *social* science; it is a science dealing with man. Inherent in this is the fact that economics must deal with moral issues; it must deal with issues which arouse passions. But economists regard any passion or emotion as a weakness; they brand such aspects as unscientific.

When the social sciences try to imitate the physical sciences too closely, they overlook precisely those qualities pertaining to *man,* such as free will and morality. That is not true science, but it is very dismal. Free will and moral issues must be taken into consideration in any study of man. They are facts.

This book is about economics; but it is not dismal. It tells about a small group of men who depreciate the nation's currency through their control of the money system—and thereby steal billions of dollars from the common people of this country. It talks about justice. And it talks about the evils which are yet to follow from this system if it is not destroyed.

So, dear reader, the author must offer an "apology." This will not be the typical dispassionate, pseudo-scientific, dismal economics book. It should not be disparaged for that reason. True science proceeds by reason and common sense. If the conclusions reached are also passionate, so be it. The Dismal Science has not achieved any great success.

CHAPTER I

A Great Forsaking

Also, I heard the voice of the Lord, saying, Whom shall I send, and who will go for us? Then said I, Here am I; send me. And he said, Go, and tell this people,

Hear and hear, but do not understand/see and see, but do not perceive,/Make the heart of this people fat,/and their ears heavy,/ and shut their eyes;/lest they see with their eyes,/and hear with their ears,/and understand with their hearts,/and turn and be healed.

Then said I, Lord, how long? And he answered, Until the cities be wasted without inhabitant, and the houses without man, and the land be utterly desolate, And the Lord have removed men far away, and there be a great forsaking in the midst of the land (Isaiah vi.8-12).

America in the last quarter of the 20th century needs a modern Isaiah, someone to warn of an impending catastrophe. The path of a human society can always be changed; but our society has

1

embarked on a course of action that can only lead to its complete destruction. Unless decisions which have already been made are reversed and present policies are changed, the average American can look forward to a life, circa 1990-2000, quite different from the lives of past generations of Americans.

He can expect to work for a giant conglomerate, so large and impersonal that in practical terms advancement depends, not on ability, but on corporate politics. He can expect that, no matter how hard he has worked during his life and no matter how carefully he has provided for his old age, he will live out his last years in poverty as a ward of the state. And in all likelihood his last years will be shortened by this poverty. He can expect that his son or his neighbor's son or his son-in-law will be conscripted and sent to die in a far-off land, in a war fabricated behind the scenes by men who will use this war to line their pockets. He can expect that his area of individual freedom will become more and more circumscribed. More and more, he will have to turn to a bureaucrat for permission to do the things which Americans have always taken for granted. Things such as; leaving the country, buying medicine, going on strike or moving into an apartment. He can expect to be threatened by a large class of drug ridden criminals every time he leaves his house at night. He can expect to find that those of his generation who become rich are the gambler and promoter types who stay one jump ahead of the law and have political connections. He can expect that social unrest will proceed to the point where a breakdown of civil order is threatened, raising the specter of anarchy. He will find that in that society of the future there will have been a reversal of the principle of justice. In that world, those who will prosper will be those who are evil; those who suffer will be those who are good.

It is hardly necessary to point out that such a society can not survive. The society of the turn of the 21st century will be a transition phase for a plunge into a cataclysm which will return civilization to a new Dark Age.

Of course, a cynic might point out that, to some extent, all of the evils predicted for the year 2000 are with us today. We have crime and drug abuse, war, giant conglomerates, government regulation, promoters and civil unrest, and our aged live in poverty.

This is true. But it is not my intention to exaggerate or alarm people about existing evils. It is my intention to warn of far greater evils to come. The evils suffered by our society today as compared with America 40 years ago are but a mild form of those which will exist in the year 2000. Today it is still possible for energetic youth to avoid serving in a war; a portion of the elderly—the most affluent 25%—can still live a reasonable old age; crime is a problem, but it is tolerable; and government regulation, while extensive, does not usually come down upon the individual in his day-to-day existence.

The mild evils we know today are all the effect of a specific cause. For the past generation that cause has been operating in a mild form. But in 1971 a fundamental change was made so that the cause is now operating in a most virulent form. Unless those decisions, made between late 1970 and late 1971, are reversed, we are going to see our society collapse about our heads.

What is happening in America today is that we are seeing the formation of an aristocratic class—a new power structure which will be to the America of the future (if indeed our descendants of the 21st century live in a place called the United States of America) as the ancient king and feudal lords who ruled society at that time were to the Dark and Middle Ages.

An aristocracy is a small elite who, through control of the government, have obtained special privileges in law and are thus enabled to live as parasites on the labor of others; by means of this exploitation they amass large amounts of unearned wealth. By this definition there is already an aristocracy in existence in America. But it has not yet consolidated its power and does not yet dare to come out in the open.

The English and American revolutions of the 17th and 18th centuries proclaimed the ideal of democracy and equality. "All men are created equal," says the Declaration of Independence. These revolutions destroyed the existing aristocracies. But they did not completely close the door to the formation of an aristocracy per se. For the past two centuries the issue has been in doubt as various groups of men sought power in massive political battles which rocked the country (but are largely ignored by history).

3

In any country the power of the people is much greater than the power of a small aristocracy (or would-be aristocracy). If the people are to be ruled, they must be ruled by deception. They must accept a set of myths which rationalize and justify their oppression. In America today we have accepted such a set of myths. The fatal decisions have been made (in 1970-71). All that remains is the gradual working out of the inner logic of events to subjugate us to a new aristocracy.

The area in which this aristocracy operates is economics, in particular the realm of money. By a process of which most Americans are not even aware, their wealth is taken from them without their consent. The closest modern Americans have come to an understanding of this process is their protest against inflation. But to even call what is happening today "inflation" is to accept one of the myths.

Since every action taken by the people to protect themselves from "inflation" threatens the source of the aristocracy's wealth, it is necessary for it to prevent these actions by successive restrictions on people's freedom. History shows that the American people will not submit to this during a time of peace. Therefore, it becomes necessary to manufacture continual wars and threats of war in order to appeal to people's patriotism, to put up with the "inflation" and the controls for the "temporary" emergency.

Thus is Isaiah's warning applicable to modern America. We "do not understand." And because of that, there will be a "great forsaking" in this country. Unless the present policies are changed, death and destruction are going to rain down upon America such as we now can not conceive.

I can not claim to have been sent by the Lord; but I do have an understanding of economics and can explain the mechanics of the corruption which is enveloping our society. Let us hope that the hearts of modern Americans will be thin, their ears light and their eyes open so that they may come to an understanding of this injustice. Then we will proceed to an action program to prevent this calamity and establish an economic system in which each man can keep for himself the product of his own labor.

CHAPTER II

Paper Money

There are two kinds of people in America today—those who have the privilege of creating money and those who have the obligation to accept it. The privilege of creating money is given to a special elite, those who own or control banks. Since it is illegal for an outsider to go into the banking business, those already in that business have a special privilege in law denied to the rest of the people. You can best understand how money operates in our modern world—how bankers profit from the system without producing any wealth, how they exploit the working people of the society, and why they have come to have special privileges in law—by examining the history of how paper money came into being.

In England, prior to about 1660, there was no paper money. Money was gold or silver coin. However, this was not honest money. The King was in the habit of taking the gold which came in to him and shaving a little bit off from each coin and passing the new coins off as equal in value to the old. Alternatively, he would melt the coins down and dilute the gold with copper and mint new coins of the same size but with less gold content. If people refused to accept these diminished coins at equal value with the original coins, then the courts (appointed by the King) would rule that the value of money came, not from the objective value of the metal, but from the declaration of the King; i.e., that the money was worth whatever the King said it was worth.

These rulings by the kings' courts were called legal tender rulings; that is, they determined just what could legally be tendered (given) in payment. The shaved or adulterated money was called fiat money because its value came from the fiat of the king.

As a product of the Reformation there began the widespread accumulation of wealth, and, starting after 1660, some people began to look for places of safekeeping. The practice started of taking one's gold to a goldsmith and paying him a small fee to keep it safe. The goldsmith in turn would issue the owner of the gold a receipt, a small slip of paper promising to return his gold upon demand. The process was the same as baggage checking today.

But unlike baggage receipts, the gold receipts soon came to have a special use. If customer Charles wanted to make a purchase from merchant Michael, then what was the sense of Charles taking his paper receipt to the goldsmith, changing it for gold, and then coming back to make the transaction? It was easier for Charles merely to pay for the merchandise with the paper receipts. Then Michael could take these to the goldsmith and redeem them for gold, if he wished.

Of course, by the same logic, Michael found it easier to keep the paper receipts and use them to make his purchase from wholesaler William. As long as everyone knew that the receipts were redeemable in gold on demand, there was no need to actually redeem them, and it was more convenient to handle the paper receipts than the actual gold. In this way paper receipts for money began to circulate as money itself.

The trouble started when a goldsmith noticed: "Even though people have the right to redeem their receipts for gold at any time, in actual practice, very few of them do, and these are balanced off by new deposits of gold coming in. If I print up more receipts than there is gold, no one will know about it because it never happens that everyone comes in to redeem all at once. And since the receipts circulate as money, I will have extra money." Beautiful.

And it sure beats honest work.

But the goldsmith didn't quite get away with his scheme. It was too blatantly something for nothing. It required a rather subtle refinement. People objected when the goldsmith simply printed paper receipts to add to his own wealth. But they did not know what to say when the goldsmith printed paper receipts with which to make loans. By this act of lending, the ancient goldsmith became a banker; this was the birth of modern banking.

When people objected to his printing up receipts for gold when he did not have enough gold to redeem the receipts, the goldsmith-banker would reply: "But I do not keep these receipts. I lend them out." And the borrower would say: "And I do not keep the receipts. I employ them productively in my business. And then I pay them back." And the goldsmith-banker would conclude: "And when he pays back the loan, I destroy the receipts."

But what the goldsmith-banker has failed to mention is that he has profited from the interest on the loan. As William Paterson said in his plan for the creation of the Bank of England, "The Bank hath benefit of interest on all moneys which it creates out of nothing."[1] This profit was unearned wealth, a gain made at the expense of the rest of the community, which lost what the banker gained.

Unfortunately, the people of this time did not understand interest. Economists and theologians, following the teachings of Aristotle and the Bible, condemned all interest as unearned wealth. But since interest was essential to the newly developing capitalist economy which was growing out of the feudal system, most people just looked the other way and said, "We're going to do it anyway." It was not until the development of the Austrian theory of money and credit by Ludwig von Mises that people could understand that interest was the price one paid for the use of goods over time, that everyone had a *time* preference and preferred to have goods right away rather than to wait for them. In simpler terms, a man who saves gives up something because he would prefer to consume his wealth immediately. The saver also confers a benefit to the man to whom he lends his savings because the latter can employ the capital which has been saved to produce additional wealth. Interest is the reward to the saver. It

7

compensates him for his act of giving up, and it is a fair price for the borrower to pay for the use of wealth-producing capital.

But while this applies to *real* capital, which has been earned and saved, it does not apply to the paper receipts printed up by the goldsmith-bankers. They did no saving; they did no giving up. Their interest represents what the medieval clerics thought all interest represented—unearned wealth. Since the people of the 17th century did not understand capital and interest, they were not able to distinguish between real capital and valid interest on the one hand and bank created "capital" and invalid interest on the other.

In the late 18th century it was common practice for a banker to print four times as many paper receipts as he had gold. This means that if a commercial banker received $1,000 in deposits, he was likely to print $4,000 in receipts. If his interest rate on loans was 7%, then he did not get 7% x $1,000 = $70; he received 7% x $4,000 = $280. His real rate of interest was 28%!

One of the real big-time bankers was the aforementioned William Paterson. Paterson got some friends together and raised £72,000 in gold and silver to lend to the King of England, who needed the money to fight a war. But instead of lending him the money directly, Paterson formed a bank and printed up paper receipts to the tune of 16-2/3 times his gold and silver. He thus lent £1,200,000 to the King, and at an interest rate of 8-1/3% per year, received interest payments of *£100,000* per year.[2] Here was a man whose total capital amounted to £72,000, and his annual interest payments were £100,000. This was a real rate of interest of almost 140% per year.

But Paterson had gone too far. It was true that most of the people would circulate the receipts and not demand gold. But there were always a few people who would. And since Paterson had only 6% as much gold as he needed, rumors began to circulate that he could not make redemption. Thus, two years after his bank was opened people came to him in large numbers and demanded redemption of their paper receipts. Paterson could not pay. He did not have enough gold.

But Paterson had had the political foresight to lend *his* paper receipts to the government. Since the paper receipts were needed to fight the war, the government could not allow them to fail (as happened to other goldsmith-bankers of the day). Paterson's paper receipts were declared to be legal tender. They were held by law to be just the same as the gold for which they had stood. Thus was born a new kind of fiat money—paper money.

The old fiat money had been adulterated metal, for example, 50% gold and 50% copper which was declared by legal tender enactments to have the value of 100% gold. It, at least, had the virtue of having partial value. But paper money has *no* objective value. Its total worth is declared by fiat and enforced by the power of the state. When people are left free to choose their own money, they choose a commodity of objective value. For reasons pertaining to the chemical characteristics of these metals, the most common choices are gold and silver. In order to get people to accept paper money government must force them to accept it by legal tender laws.

The first bankers had operated on the basis of fraud. They promised to redeem in gold more paper notes than they could actually redeem. They remained in business only so long as people did not ask them to keep their promises. But with William Paterson, we can see the basic elements which constitute our present aristocracy. The banker is constituted a special elite person; he is given the privilege in law of having his paper receipts declared to be legal tender money; and by this means, he acquires an unearned wealth.

This is the origin and basic essence of bank created paper money. However, the system has undergone a considerable evolution to arrive at its modern form. You have not been taught this in history class, but the major political issue which has occupied this country since its inception has been the issue of hard money, of objective value, versus bank-created paper money.

From the time of its discovery, paper money was extensively used in America, especially in connection with wars. Its most famous use was the Continental currency of the Revolutionary War. But after this currency had become worthless and the people had stopped using it, Congress sent Thomas Jefferson on an inquiry to create a currency for the new country.

Jefferson reported that the people had already adopted a

currency, the Spanish dollar (or piece of eight), a gold or silver coin in common use in the Spanish colonies. Congress then adopted this coin as the official money of the country, and, a few years later when the Constitution was written, prohibited the enactment of legal tender laws.

The liberal, equalitarian viewpoint of the Founding Fathers had led them to an extreme hard money point of view. But the bankers were not ready to give up. They had suffered a defeat with the establishment of an official gold/silver standard at the time of the writing of the Constitution. But they still retained the privilege of issuing paper receipts, called bank notes, far in excess of any gold or silver they had in their vaults with which to redeem them. Typically, bankers would issue more and more paper notes to maximize their profits. It was a matter of delicate judgement as to how many notes one could issue before the public would become alarmed and demand their gold. Periodically, the more greedy members of the fraternity would issue to excess. Then there would be a run on that bank's gold; it would not be able to pay; and it would collapse.

The first attempt by the bankers to expand their power was Hamilton's proposal for a central bank. A central bank is one along the lines of William Paterson's institution. It is accorded a special status by the government, and its primary function is to make the government loans. Bankers found that a central bank offered them the following advantage. When a small bank got itself into trouble by an overissue of bank notes and suffered a run on its gold, the central bank would step in and lend the small bank gold to tide it over the run. Thus protected by the central bank, the small banks, who had previously expanded their note issue to three to five times their gold, now felt safe to expand it substantially beyond that, with correspondingly greater profits.

Jefferson, who understood the economic and political implications of banking, was, in principle, a foe of all bank note expansion. As he stated in a letter to Dr. Thomas Cooper on Jan. 16, 1814: "Everything predicted by the enemies of banks, in the beginning is now coming to pass. We are to be ruined now by the deluge of bank paper, as we were formerly by the old Continental paper. It is cruel that such revolutions in private fortunes should be at the mercy of avaricious adventurers, who instead of employing their capital, if any they have, in manufacturers, commerce and other useful pursuits, make it an instrument to burden all the interchanges of property with their swindling profits, profits which are the price of no useful industry of theirs. Prudent men must be on their guard in this game of *Robin's Alive,* and take care that the spark does not extinguish in their hands. I am an enemy to all banks discounting bills or notes for anything but coin."[3] Jefferson was unsuccessful in stopping the banks in the practice of issuing notes in excess of their gold, but he decided to fight Hamilton on the issue of central banking, which allows a far greater expansion of note issue. This fight between the conservative forces, led by Hamilton, and the liberal forces, led first by Jefferson and then by Van Buren and Jackson, was the major political issue of the early 19th century (1791 to 1835). The Jeffersonian forces were ultimately successful when Andrew Jackson vetoed the extension of the central bank's charter and was widely supported by the populace. However, the basic idea of the evil of bank paper, per se, had not been communicated so the nation wound up in the position of opposing central banking without really knowing why.

In addition to the use of notes, banking was refined another step with the system of writing checks (officially called demand deposits to distinguish them from savings or time deposits). Just as the banks could issue more notes than they had gold, so they could create more money in checking accounts than they had notes. Banking became a structure of pyramids. At the base was gold, the real money. On top of that were three, four or five times the quantity of bank notes printed on the assumption that only a few people would turn them in for gold. And on top of that were several times the quantity of demand deposits, created on the assumption that only a few people would cash in their checks for bank notes.

The structure of banking in three phases is shown in the charts on pages 12 and 13. Note that banking has always depended on creating money in excess of its cash. Modern bankers, however, have the advantage that for them cash is Federal Reserve notes. Thus their cash can be increased at the will of the Fed.

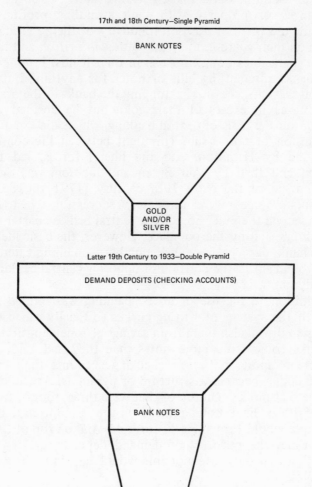

BANKING AS A STRUCTURE OF PYRAMIDS

17th and 18th Century—Single Pyramid

BANK NOTES

GOLD
AND/OR
SILVER

Latter 19th Century to 1933—Double Pyramid

DEMAND DEPOSITS (CHECKING ACCOUNTS)

BANK NOTES

GOLD
AND/OR
SILVER

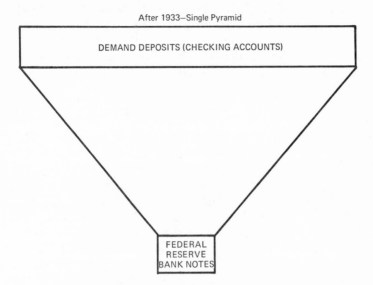

BANKING AS A STRUCTURE OF PYRAMIDS

After 1933–Single Pyramid

DEMAND DEPOSITS (CHECKING ACCOUNTS)

FEDERAL
RESERVE
BANK NOTES

This explains the nature of banking as it developed in the 17th and 18th centuries. To relate this to our modern system of money you must understand three additional developments:

(1) The establishment of a uniform national currency. By this act, passed during the Civil War, the notes of all banks were required to be standardized. (Also, Treasury bills, whose redemption later became the responsibility of the government, were issued.) It was the standardization imposed by this act which allowed the bankers to later claim that their paper notes were dollars. In legal and economic fact at this time a dollar was a quantity of gold (or silver). Modern Americans do not understand that a dollar was originally a unit of weight, like an ounce or a ton. (It was, in fact, 25.8 grains of gold, 9/10 fine.) The paper notes which passed in circulation were merely receipts for dollars. But when these notes became standardized, the bankers began to refer to the notes as dollars, a fact which ultimately eased the transition to paper money.

(2) The creation of a central bank. In the year 1900, the country was solidly against the institution of a central bank, but as has

been noted it was Jeffersonian in form without really understanding the essence of what Jefferson had been saying. A group of bankers were therefore able to put across the enactment of a central bank by sophisticatedly disguising it as a bank reform measure and then feigning opposition to their own proposal. This central bank was the Federal Reserve System (actually a system of 12 banks) created in 1913. The Federal Reserve immediately began to act very much like William Paterson's original central bank. That is, it expanded the note issue and lent the money to the government to fight a war. The results were big profits for the bankers.

Two important differences between the creation of the Federal Reserve System and the creation of William Paterson's Bank of England should be noted. Paterson created his bank in competition with and in opposition to the smaller private banks, and in fact the first rumors concerning the solvency of his bank were spread by jealous smaller bankers. But the Federal Reserve has never been in competition with American private bankers; it is controlled by the private bankers and is used to serve their interests. Also, Paterson found his war and took advantage of it. But the banking element which manipulated the Federal Reserve System through an economically naive Congress was a major reason for U.S. entry into World War I.

(3) The declaration of paper money as a legal tender. After the bankers had lent their notes to the Government to finance World War I, they turned and lent to the business community, thus sparking the business boom of the 1920s. (The effect of bank paper in creating booms and depressions will be discussed in Chapters III and IV.) This note issue reached its peak in 1929 when the banks found themselves overextended and were forced to contract. In the period 1929-1933 there were runs on banks with people demanding their gold. These runs reached a climax with the bank holiday of 1933. At that time the Federal Reserve System did what William Paterson had done in 1696; it refused to redeem its notes for gold. The Government then declared bank notes of the Federal Reserve System to be a legal tender. This was the creation of paper money in the United States.[4]

In our present banking system the first pyramid is gone.

Standardized Federal Reserve notes have replaced the standardized private bank notes, and since the former are a legal tender, there is no need to back them with gold (although the nation still maintains a gold supply). However, the second pyramid remains, and the nation's banks now expand their demand deposits on a base of Federal Reserve notes.

With the enactment of a legal tender law in 1933, the basic system was created which is now leading to the formation of an American aristocracy. The bankers and the Federal Reserve have, since that time, used their privilege to create a quarter of a trillion paper dollars. The interest which they have charged on this money represents wealth stolen from the American people. This is the basis of the system. It is to protect this income-producing privilege that the bankers are forced to expand their power and constitute themselves an aristocratic class.

In the early days of paper money, profiteers and adventurers arose who exploited the system for all it was worth. You will find the story of Andrew Dexter, Jr., as reported in the "Democratic Press" in 1809, an interesting example:

Each revolving year brings forth some extraordinary novelty to excite wonder and gratify curiosity. Long as banks have been in operation in various parts of the world, it was reserved for the present age, so fertile in discoveries and improvements, to invent the *ne plus ultra* of liberality and accommodation in the tenor of a promissory note. And the most remarkable feature in this affair, is that the discovery was not made in London, Paris, Vienna, Philadelphia, New York, or Boston, but in a two-penny village, called Gloucester, in Rhode Island, containing about a dozen houses. In this village, immortalized by the invention, there was a bank established in 1805, of which the capital was composed of two thousand shares, of fifty dollars each, amounting to 100,000 dollars. Of this bank, Andrew Dexter, Junr. an illustrious speculator, borrowed the trivial sum of 845,771 dollars in their bank notes, for which sum he gave his promissory notes, without indorser, in the following improved form:

"I Andrew Dexter, Junr. do promise the President, Directors, and company of the Farmer's Exchange Bank, to pay them, or order _____ dollars, in _____ years, from the date, with interest *at two per cent per annum;* it being, however, understood that the said Dexter shall not be called upon to make payment *until he thinks proper;* he being the principle stockholder, and *best knowing when it will be proper to pay the same.*"

I annex the amount of the respective notes and the periods of payment, for the gratification of the reader:

1. One dated Nov. 4, 1808 at		
eight years and 2 per cent for	Dolls.	300,000
2. One dated Nov. 30, 1808, for		32,000
3. One dated Dec. 12, 1808,		6,000
4. One dated Nov. 30, 1808,		507,771
		845,771

With the bank notes received by Dexter for these notes of hand, there was carried on a stupendous scene of fraud and villainy. They were employed in the purchase of property of every kind, by Dexter and his friends: and as they made no scruple about price, they possessed themselves of many of the most valuable estates in New England, some of which had descended from father to son since the first settlement of the country. Hundreds, perhaps thousands of people deplore their fatal credulity, which induced them to convert their property into this paper, not now worth a cent on the dollar, which has reduced them from a state of affluence to beggary and wretchedness.

The bank ceased its operations on the 27th of February, 1809, with the enormous sum of specie in its vaults of eighty-six dollars and fifty cents, which on accurate calculation, will probably pay a farthing in the hundred dollars to his creditors.

The legislature of Rhode-Island at its last session appointed a committee to investigate the whole of the nefarious transaction. The committee has published a luminous report for the information of their constitutents, from which this sketch is taken.[5]

Such abuses outraged the public, and bankers realized that some limitations on their note issues were necessary if the privilege were not to be denied them altogether. Therefore, regulations were passed limiting the amount of notes a bank could print in relation to its gold. These regulations continue today except that today they limit the amount of demand deposits a bank can create in relation to its Federal Reserve notes. Abuses such as the above also show why banking has been limited to a special elite. If everyone could create money, then everyone would, and the system would break down.

Bank profits today thus depend heavily on the actions of the Federal Reserve. If the Federal Reserve issues more notes, then banks can use these notes as a base on which to expand their demand deposits, which they do in a manner similar to the ancient goldsmith by making loans. These additional loans bring in additional interest, which is profitable for the bank. In our modern world the Federal Reserve is very important for the banks. It can make or lose them millions of dollars. The Federal Reserve in our modern society has the magical power to create money. It simply prints a note, and since its notes are legal tender, presto, it has created money.

In theory the Federal Reserve might print money for any purpose. The head of the Federal Reserve might go into a restaurant, order a steak dinner and then print up a Federal Reserve note to pay for it. But traditionally the central bank has existed primarily for the purpose of lending the government money. In practice the only time the Federal Reserve prints money is when the Federal Government runs a budget deficit and needs to borrow.

When the Federal budget is in deficit, the U.S. Treasury prints up pieces of paper called Government Bonds. A bond is nothing more than an IOU. Then the Federal Reserve prints up pieces of paper called Federal Reserve notes. A note is nothing but an IOU. Then these two agencies exchange IOUs.[6] But since the legal tender laws are deemed to have the magical power to make pieces of paper into money, presto, money has been created.

This is how the Federal Government borrows money in our present society. In reality our Government is bankrupt. The people do not have enough confidence in the Government to lend it money. Were it not for the Federal Reserve the Government could not borrow enough to meet the huge deficits it runs. But the important thing to understand is that every time the Federal Reserve creates money to lend to the Government, that money finds its way into the banking system. (That is, it is spent, goes into circulation, and is deposited in a bank.) Then it can be used as a base upon which to multiply the bank's loans (demand deposits).

According to present regulations (depending on the type of bank) demand deposits can be increased by more than six times the cash base; thus, for every dollar printed by the Federal Reserve, the banks can create five times that amount in loans, receiving corresponding interest payments.

Banks, therefore, have a vested interest (in more than one sense) in budget deficits. Since by far the biggest budget deficits occur during war, banks have a vested interest in war.

FOOTNOTES

[1] William Paterson, as quoted by Eric D. Butler, *The Enemy Within the Empire, A Short History of the Bank of England* [Melbourne, 194], p. 3.

[2] The facts concerning the establishment of the Bank of England are surely among the most obscure in economic history. The source of these is a pamphlet entitled *Remarks Upon the Bank of England, With Regard More Especially to Our Trade and Government. Occasion'd by the Present Discourse Concerning the Intended Prolongation of the Bank. Humbly Address'd to the Honourable House of Commons.* by a Merchant of London, and a True Lover of Our Constitution (London, Printed for A. Baldwin, in Warwick-Lane, 1706), and Charles Holt Carroll, "Banking and Credit Systems, II," *The Organization of Debt Into Currency and Other Papers,* ed. Edward C. Simons (Princeton, N.J., 1964), originally published in *Hunt's Merchants' Magazine and Commercial Review,* XXIX, (Oct. 1858), pp. 443-50.

[3] Thomas Jefferson, *Writings,* Monticello Ed. (Washington, D.C., 1905), XIV, p. 61.

[4] I include in this private bank deposits with the Federal Reserve. These are also Fed. obligations and may easily be converted into the form of paper notes.

[5] "Democratic Press" [1809], as quoted by Benjamin Davies, *The Bank Torpedo* (New York, 1810), pp. 57-59.

[6] The exchange is usually indirect.

CHAPTER III

Who Gains And Who Loses?

If banks profit from paper money, you may be asking: Who loses? This is an important question because some economists go so far as to contend that no one loses. This is absurd on the face of it. If one segment of the population is receiving values without producing anything in exchange, then it follows that someone else must be producing without getting the product of his labor.

But if one analyzes the situation purely in terms of flows of money, it seems as though these economists are right. The banker, of course, has more money; it is he who has issued it. The businessman to whom he has made the loan benefits; the existence of more loanable funds through this process has meant that he is able to get his loan at a lower rate of interest. In addition, when the businessman starts his project, he employs more workers; so these workers benefit. As the additional money gets spent and flows into the economy of the surrounding area, the people of this area accumulate more money. Everyone gains; no one loses.

This essential theory, in various forms, has continually resurfaced again and again in history. Shortly after our country was established, there was a revolution in the state of Massachusetts called Shays' Rebellion which advocated general prosperity by paper money. The idea was that government should run a large budget deficit, which would be financed by printing paper money. To increase the deficit, it was advocated to abolish taxes and to spend money on public works.

The fallacy involved in this argument consists of analyzing what happens only in terms of money. Since the essence of the paper money scheme is to create more money, then when measured in terms of money, everyone has more. What must be remembered is that money is not wealth. Money is just a means to facilitate exchange. King Midas had all the money he wanted, but it did him no good because he could not even eat an apple.

The advocates of bank paper praise it because, they say, it gives the businessman more capital, and capital is productive. Capital creates additional wealth. But it is important to distinguish between money capital and real capital. Money capital are pieces of paper in a vault or notations on a ledger. Real capital are steam shovels, which can help dig the foundation for a building; trucks, which help carry goods to market; and labor saving machinery, which increases the productivity of workers. Real capital is productive. Real capital increases the quantity of wealth in the world.

But the increased issue of bank paper does not increase real capital. It only increases money capital. When the banks create money to loan to businessmen, these businessmen use the additional money to bid capital away from other members of the community. Let us consider a simple example: There is a small community with ten farmers and one bank. The bank wants the extra profits from paper money so it persuades one of the farmers, more "enterprising" and "forward looking" than the others, to take a loan to expand his farm. There are ten harvesting machines in this community of which the "enterprising" farmer has one. He uses his loan to buy an additional harvesting machine.

The banker, of course, has gained. He has the interest payments on the loan. In addition, the "enterprising" farmer has gained. Because the banker had additional money to loan, he lowered the rate of interest in order to induce borrowing. Before the issue of paper money the productivity of a harvesting machine was 7% of its value, and the cost of a loan was 8% interest. But now the banker has reduced the interest rate to 6%. Thus the "enterprising" farmer stands to make a gain.

In addition, by buying the additional harvester, the "enterprising" farmer has bid up the market price of harvesters. Thus all of the other farmers in the community think they are richer because their harvesters are worth more. Even the conservative farmer who sold his harvester is happy. He, after all, has sold his harvester for more than he reasonably could have expected to get for it.

But while everyone is happy, it is clear that not everyone could have gained. *In real terms* the community has exactly as much capital as it had before. There are still ten harvesters in that community. Since there is now more money in circulation but no additional goods, it will take more money to buy the same quantity of goods. The law of supply and demand has been operating on this community. Since the supply of money has increased, the value of money has gone down. This is expressed in the fact that it now takes more money to buy the same harvesting machine. The value of the currency has depreciated.

So the conservative farmer is not as smart as he thinks. He has sold his harvester for more money, but it is money of depreciated value. The eight other farmers think their harvesters are worth more; but they are only worth more in terms of depreciated money. As the extra money circulates through the community into all the channels of trade, it gradually raises the average price of goods. When the conservative farmer and the other farmers go to spend their money, they will find that they can buy less. Although in money terms they are richer, their money has depreciated; in real terms they are poorer. And the amount of their loss is (approximately) equal[1] to the gain of the banker and the "enterprising" farmer. As Jefferson said: ". . . capital may be produced by industry, and accumulated by economy; but jugglers only will propose to create it by legerdemain tricks with paper."[2]

In actuality, the mistake made by the conservative farmer is the same in kind as the mistake made by those who sold estates to Andrew Dexter, Jr. in our previous example. They sold real wealth for depreciated paper, and although the amount of money they got was higher, the value they got was lower. This example serves to illustrate a number of points:

(1) The basic thing which is going on as a result of an issue of paper money is a transfer of wealth from the community as a whole to the banker and the borrower.

(2) In this transfer, a large number of people lose a small amount, and a few gain a large amount.

(3) If we look at the transactions only in money terms, it appears as though everyone has gained.

(4) However, what has really happened is that the value of the money has depreciated. Thus in terms of money the average price of goods is higher. When people go to spend their money, they will cry: "Inflation."

In the 18th century there was a vehement debate over whether, in these circumstances, it was the value of money which was going down or the value of goods which was going up. The banking interests tried to contend that their issues of additional paper money did not cause a depreciation in the value of money. Faced with the fact that it took more money to buy the same goods they responded that it was the value of goods which had risen, with the implication that this rise in goods was spontaneous and accidental and in no way related to the extra issues of paper money.

This theory appears plausible in our present society—where honest money has been outlawed by the government and prices are only stated in terms of depreciated currency. But the War of 1812 provides a clear example of paper money and gold/silver money circulating side by side. During this war, the Southern and Western banks overexpanded their note issues to lend money to the Government, and when the war went badly, there were runs on these banks; like William Paterson in 1696, they suspended their payments of gold and silver. The New England banks, however, did not overexpand and were able to continue redeeming their notes in gold and silver. The result was that the price of goods in terms of New York or Baltimore bank notes was 10%-25% higher than their price in terms of Boston bank notes. Clearly it was the New York and Baltimore money which had depreciated in value. As Daniel Webster noted at the time:

> The depreciation of bank-notes was the necessary consequence of
> a neglect or refusal to pay them, on the part of those who issued

them. It took place immediately, and has continued, with occasional fluctuations in the depression, to the present moment. What still further increases the evil is, that this bank paper, being the issue of very many institutions, situated in different parts of the country, and possessing different degrees of credit, the depreciation has not been, and is not now, uniform throughout the United States. It is not the same at Baltimore as at Philadelphia, nor the same at Philadelphia as at New York. In New England, the banks have not stopped payment in specie, and of course their paper has not been depressed at all. . . . This difference in relation to the paper of the District where we now are, is twenty-five per cent.[3]

The propaganda of the banking forces was ultimately successful and the theory of a mysterious and accidental rise in goods unrelated to the increase in the money supply took hold. It is this theory which is implied in the word "inflation." "Inflation" means a going up. To use that word in connection with higher prices implies that goods have gone up. But when we look at the economic universe at a time of large issues of paper money we find that that is not the case. We find that values of goods bear the same relationship to each other. We find that values of goods bear the same relationship to hard money, which has not been increased in supply. We find that in the whole economic universe only one item has significantly changed its value: That is the paper money which has been issued to excess. And the value of this item in relation to all other items is down.

For this reason, the correct word to use in this circumstance is "depreciation," which means a going down. When average prices rise as a result of an issue of paper money, what is occurring is a *depreciation of the currency.*

The relationship between paper money and currency depreciation is vividly illustrated in the accompanying chart (see Illustration 1, page 24). Pro-bank economists are still trying to argue that paper money does not depreciate the currency. They do this by only focusing on the short range picture, where economic causes have not had time to show their effects or where the inadequacies of their own indicators distort their picture of reality. Study this chart carefully to see the *long term* relationship between paper

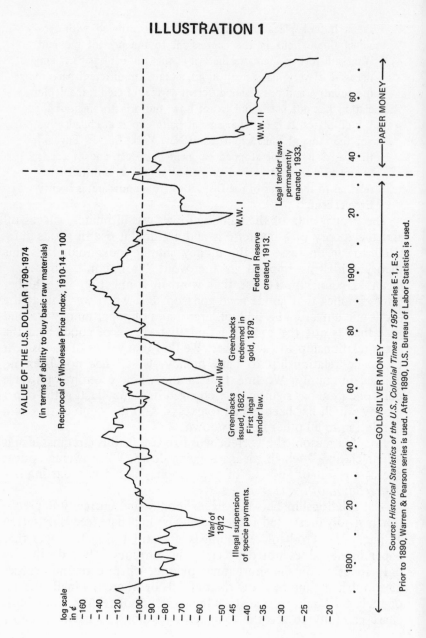

ILLUSTRATION 1

VALUE OF THE U.S. DOLLAR 1790-1974

(in terms of ability to buy basic raw materials)

Reciprocal of Wholesale Price Index, 1910-14 = 100

Source: *Historical Statistics of the U.S., Colonial Times to 1957* series E-1, E-3.
Prior to 1890, Warren & Pearson series is used. After 1890, U.S. Bureau of Labor Statistics is used.

24

money and the value of the dollar.

There were three periods of "inflation" or currency depreciation during this time; each of them was associated with a war and extra issues of paper money, and each of them saw some abrogation of the gold standard. But in each case, after the emergency, the money supply was contracted and prices declined to their previous levels. Thus, over a period of 145 years, the U.S. currency retained its value. Prices in 1933 were approximately the same as they had been 145 years earlier when the Constitution first established a gold standard.

The reason for this is simple. During this period the dollar was defined as a quantity of gold. The dollar maintained its value because gold maintained its value. And gold maintained its value because it could not simply be printed up and issued to excess like a piece of paper. In fact gold was chosen as money by people because, of all the economic goods circulating in human commerce, it has the best record for maintaining its value.

But since the enactment of a legal tender law in 1933, there has been a continual depreciation of the currency. Since that time the dollar has been defined, not as a quantity of gold, but as a piece of paper declared to have value by the fiat of the state.

In addition to the direct benefit to the banker, who issues the paper money, and the benefit to the debtor, who receives the loan, the depreciation associated with the paper money also sets up additional imbalances in the regular path of commerce:

(1) The real value of your wages declines in a period of currency depreciation. In a free economy, prices are always fluctuating in response to supply and demand. But some prices are more responsive than others. The prices of vegetables in your local supermarket and stocks in the stock market are extremely responsive and change within a few minutes or a few days. On the other hand, the price of a piece of real estate may not change for years. It happens that wages are more like real estate in this regard. History shows they are slower to change in response to changes in the value of the currency than prices. In a period of currency depreciation, prices will move up before wages, and in a period of currency appreciation, prices will move down before wages. The following statistics illustrate this fact.[4] (See tables on pages 26-27.)

Civil War currency depreciation—change from 1861

	Wholesale price index	Wages
1862	+17%	+3%
1863	+49%	+18.1%
1864	+117%	+33.3%

The sharp rise in prices early in the Civil
War was not matched by the rise in wages.

Civil War currency appreciation—change from 1864

	Wholesale price index	Wages
1865	-4%	+11.8%
1866	-10%	+16.1%
1867	-16%	+22.4%

But wages kept going up after the war and caught up.

World War I currency depreciation—change from 1915

	Wholesale price index	Wages
1916	+23%	+11.5%
1917	+69%	+26.8%
1918	+89%	+49.3%

And the same thing happened in WWI
But wages began to catch up in 1919 and 1920.

World War I currency appreciation—change from 1920

	Wholesale price index	Wages
1921	-37%	-8%

And they really caught up in 1921 by only slipping
a little in the face of a major price decline.

Great Depression—change from 1929

	Wholesale price index	Wages
1930	-9.3%	0%
1931	-23.4%	-4.4%
1932	-32%	-15.4%

In the Great Depression, prices fell more rapidly than wages.

Silver demonetization currency appreciation—change from 1882

	Wholesale price index	Wages
1883	-6.5%	+4.1%
1884	-14%	+1.4%
1885	-21.2%	+2%

And in a price decline in the 1880's, wages didn't
fall at all but merely rose less rapidly.

Thus, in the early stages of a currency depreciation, the prices you pay will rise faster than your wages. The businessman then benefits from a period in which the prices he charges for his goods go up while the wages he pays his workers either remain the same or go up much more slowly. This is a truth which seems to have been forgotten today as people are blaming labor for the present "inflation." But it was widely recognized in previous times. As President Cleveland said: "At times like the present, when the evils of unsound finance threaten us, the speculator may anticipate a harvest gathered from the misfortune of others, the capitalist may protect himself by hoarding or may even find profit in the fluctuation of values; but the wage earner—the first to be injured by a depreciated currency and the last to receive the benefit of its correction—is practically defenseless."[5] Even Keynes recognized this when he said: "When money-wages are rising, this is to say, it will be found that real wages are falling; and when money-wages are falling, real wages are rising."[6] So, as the currency depreciates, the employer benefits at the expense of the employee.

(2) Debtors gain at the expense of creditors. We have already

27

seen how debtors are enabled to borrow money at lower rates of interest due to the surplus lending power of the banks (as in the case of the "enterprising" farmer). But an additional benefit to debtors from paper money lies in the fact that they are enabled to pay their debts in depreciated currency.

A debtor who borrows $1,000 may pay back the same nominal sum. But if the currency has depreciated 20% in the interval, then he is only paying back $800 in real terms. A debtor who borrowed $1,000 in 1861, when the dollar was 25.8 grains of gold, was borrowing 25,800 grains of gold. If he paid his debt in legal tender greenbacks (issued to help fight the Civil War) in 1864, at a time when the dollar had depreciated 50% in terms of gold, then he paid back 12,900 grains of gold. This meant that he had a profit of $500.

(3) The unscrupulous gain at the expense of the gullible. You have already seen how an infusion of paper money into a community makes everyone at first think they are richer. As a result, many people purchase luxury items, which they can not properly afford, and a favorite luxury item is a fling in the stock or commodity markets. Every period of paper money expansion has seen some type of bubble whereby large numbers of naive newcomers enter the speculative markets hoping to make a lot of money. To accommodate these people, there arise fast buck operators who are always handy with schemes for instant riches. Starting with the Mississippi bubble and the South Sea bubble to the recent "new breed" (who rose to make profits from the paper money associated with the Vietnam War), every period of paper money expansion has seen some type of emotional mania on the markets. When the dust has lifted from these manias and the overinflated stocks have collapsed down to their true values, it can be seen that there has been a large transfer of wealth from the gullible newcomers to the fast buck operators who promoted the schemes which took them in.

We are now at a point where we can understand what happens when paper money is issued. Some people do gain something for nothing, but this is counterbalanced by a loss to the great majority of people, a loss which shows up in a depreciation of the currency, which the average person calls inflation. This loss can not be seen by examining money. In terms of money, everyone gains. It can only be seen by examining real wealth.

To summarize, there are those who lose and those who gain from paper money. Bankers gain from paper money, of course, because it is they who issue it. This gain is made at the expense of the rest of the community, which suffers from the depreciation of the currency.

Business, especially big business, gains from paper money in three ways. First, since wages are slower to rise than prices in response to the depreciation, the real wages of labor go down. Business benefits because in real terms it is paying lower wages. Second, it is not widely known, but the major debtors in our society (or any society) are the big businesses. An individual or a small business is not as good a credit risk as a large corporation and cannot go as deeply into debt. In its capacity as a borrower, business benefits because the creation of paper loanable funds reduces the rate of interest below what it otherwise would have been. When the rate of interest is artificially lowered, all debtors benefit at the expense of those who save (primarily the middle class). Lastly, business also benefits in its capacity as a borrower because, in a period of currency depreciation, it is enabled to pay off its debts in money of lower value.

Promoters and fast buck operators, the hangers-on of any paper money scheme, take advantage of the gullible to create an emotional turbulance on the markets.

As against these, the vast majority of people in the society lose. In particular, the elderly in a society suffer from the depreciation of the currency. It is they who have put away money for their old age. As this money depreciates in value, they are reduced to poverty. For example, in 1960 it was not unreasonable for a 50-year-old man to plan retirement on a $3,000 annual income. But now, as retirement approaches, how much will $3,000 buy? $3,000 is now below the poverty line. And if the "inflation" continues until 1985, how much will $3,000 buy then?

The middle class also lose. Like the elderly, they lose from the depreciation of their savings. However, they also lose from the artificial lowering of the rate of interest. Since it is they who are the most thrifty and do the real saving (saving of real capital), it is they who lose most from a depressed interest rate.

And of course, the worker loses as his wages do not keep pace with the depreciation of the currency.

FOOTNOTES

[1] It is actually greater because the process involves waste. This will be discussed below.

[2] Thomas Jefferson, letter to John W. Eppes, Nov. 6, 1813, *Writings,* XIII, p. 423.

[3] Daniel Webster, "The Legal Currency," speech delivered in the House of Representatives, April 26, 1816, *The Debates and Proceedings in the Congress of the United States, Fourteenth Congress—First Session* (Washington, D.C., 1854), pp. 1441-42.

[4] Historical Statistics of the United States, Colonial Times to 1957 (Washington, 1960) Wholesale Price Index—series E 1-24; wages prior to 1890—series D 573; wages WW I—series D590, average hourly earnings in manufacturing; wages depression—series D 654, average hourly earnings in 25 manufacturing industries.

[5] Grover Cleveland, "Annual Message to Congress—1888," as quoted in *The Great Quotations,* compiled by George Seldes (New York, 1960), p. 163.

[6] John Maynard Keynes, *General Theory of Employment, Interest and Money* (London, 1936), [rights controlled by Harcourt Brace Jovanovich, Inc.] p. 10.

CHAPTER IV

Modern Theology

We have thus established that a special elite exists in this country which is given the special privilege in law of creating money. And you have seen how this privilege enables them, and a larger group who benefit from their actions, to gain wealth at the expense of the vast majority of Americans.

But the elite faces a problem common to all aristocracies. How does a small minority exploit a large majority? If the exploiters were a majority, their portion would not be large enough to be of much value. But if physical force is the criterion, then the majority can easily overwhelm a small minority.

The way aristocracies have solved this problem in the past is by deception. They create a set of myths which justify their superior position and convince the majority to accept its own exploitation. The aristocracies of the Middle Ages preached the doctrine that some men were by birth superior to others and that God had established this as a natural order. Resistance to the aristocracy was resistance to God. Submission, even to unjust rulers, was required by the teachings of religion and would be rewarded in the afterlife.

So, too, our modern banker elite and its associated vested interests in big business preach a set of myths, a set of myths which is unquestioned in the social controversy of our time and which rationalizes and justifies their special position.

These are:

(1) A paper money expansion is not merely the good of a special interest. It is a general good which benefits everyone. Conversely, a contraction is an unmitigated evil with no good to anyone.

(2) The real reason policies of paper money expansion are advocated is out of a sense of altruism. This is done for the benefit of the poor and unfortunate.

(3) Paper money has the magical effect of creating something out of nothing. This is why we are all better off from its use.

Myth 1. The myth of the general good.

In the 18th and 19th centuries when the proponents and opponents of paper money waged their battles, it was taken for granted that there were two contending classes—generally styled debtors and creditors (although as we have seen, the actual classes are more inclusive than that)—and that when one gained the other would lose. But today there is no such conception. Today, the effects of paper money expansion are called a business boom and are held to be good for all. The effects of contraction are called a depression and are held to be a universal evil. For this reason let us now turn to a more careful examination of the business boom. (See Illustration 2 on page 33.)

The period 1965-1969 was a period of economic boom. By all the traditional indices, the economy was expanding. Gross National Product was up. Industrial production was up. Unemployment was down. The large majority of business indicators were up. But during that period take-home pay of the average worker in terms of real buying power declined. Note that it is normal for real wages to rise. From the post WW II period to 1965, real wages increased by over 40%. In the great period of declining prices from 1865 to 1900, real wages of the average American worker more than doubled. (See Illustration 3 on page 43 for chart of real take-home pay.)

ILLUSTRATION 2

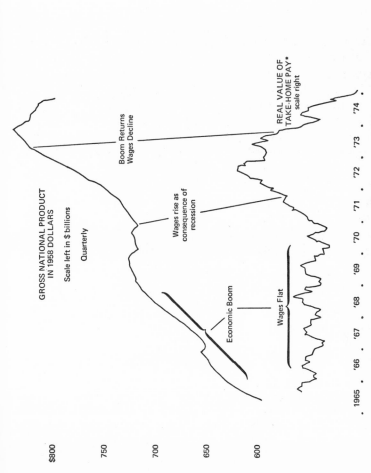

GROSS NATIONAL PRODUCT
IN 1958 DOLLARS

Scale left in $ billions

Quarterly

Economic Boom

Wages Flat

Wages rise as
consequence of
recession

Boom Returns
Wages Decline

REAL VALUE OF
TAKE-HOME PAY*
scale right

$800

750

700

650

600

1965 · '66 · '67 · '68 · '69 · '70 · '71 · '72 · '73 · '74 ·

98 · 96 · 94 · 92 · 90 · 88 · 86 ·

*Spendable average weekly earnings of production or non-supervisory workers on private non-agricultural payrolls. Monthly, worker with three dependents $ of 1967 value. Source, U.S. Bureau of Labor Statistics, "Employment and Earnings" #1312.9 Does not include deductions for State and City income taxes and other local deductions from weekly paychecks. (The Bureau of Labor Statistics has tried several times to drop this index.)

33

To one educated in our modern society, this is a startling fact. But fact it is and the surprise you feel is only a measure of the success of the banking aristocracy in having convinced virtually everyone of a falsehood. While we have been told that we are better off and are getting richer, in fact we have been getting poorer!

In 1968, in the middle of the boom, dozens of fast buck operators were making money hand over fist. What was known on Wall Street as the "new breed"—men like Bernard Cornfeld, Howard Levin and James Ling—were living high, wide and handsome; but the average American was finding that, by a process he did not quite understand, his paycheck bought less and less at the supermarket each week.

What is happening in the U.S. economy is that there are two groups, one of which is exploiting the other. These are the groups defined in the last chapter; the banks, big business and their entourage of gamblers and promoters on the one hand; and the middle class and working class, especially the elderly, on the other. This is the conflict recognized by Jefferson and characterized by him as the banks and the big corporations versus the common man. In general terms the characterization is accurate. The business statistics which define boom and recession are not indices which measure the general wealth of the economy as a whole. These indices go up when there is a transfer of wealth from the second group to the first. They go down when the transfer slows or stops or goes into reverse. They measure not the general good but the exploitation of one social class by another.

For example, high corporate profits, a rising stock market and falling interest rates are all used by economists to indicate a booming economy. Yet all three of these indices measure the gain of the paper money clique at the expense of others.

When a currency depreciation increases prices faster than wages, then business profits will increase, and the stock market will go up, but this will not measure a gain for the whole society; it will merely measure gains made by business at the expense of the worker-consumer. Similarly, when interest rates fall, then business profits will increase because one of business' important costs (the cost of borrowing) will be lowered. But this does not represent a gain for society as a whole. It simply represents a transfer of wealth from lender to borrower; business benefits at the expense of the thrifty.

Many of the other commonly used indices of business are merely other ways of looking at the above three statistics. For example, an increase in housing starts is regarded as good for the economy, but an increase in housing starts is caused by and largely correlative with a drop in interest rates. Capital spending is caused by and follows rising profits and falling interest rates. These are statistics which indirectly measure what the above three directly measure— that is, the transfer of wealth from the majority of working, consuming, saving Americans to the bankers and big business.

The most commonly used index on the economy is the Gross National Product. For most students of the subject, GNP *is* the economy. For this reason, you should give this index special attention.

Suppose a bright, young inventor develops a cheaper way to produce electric power so that electric power can now be produced and sold for half the previous cost. Unquestionably this is an increase in the wealth of the community which is fortunate enough to have such a man. The people in the community can now have the same amount of power as before with more resources left over to buy other goods. But this increase in wealth in the community will not show up as an increase in the Gross National Product. In fact, since people will now spend less on electric power, the contribution to GNP by electric power will be smaller! But it is clear that people are getting the same amount of electric power as before. How then can electric power show up as less in computing GNP? And if it does, does GNP really measure the increase in wealth which has taken place? (For a detailed examination of how GNP is computed, see Appendix A.)

In general, there are only two ways in which wealth can be increased: Something which was done before can be done more effectively or efficiently; or something new can be created.

If something is done more effectively, then there will be a reduction in cost. Thus, the contribution to GNP from this source will be less. Correspondingly, people will have more money left over (the amount they saved by the reduction in cost) and will spend it on other things. Since the amount of new spending on other things equals the reduction of spending on the product in which the efficiency was discovered, the reduction in GNP from the efficiency will just equal the gain in GNP from the extra spending. Other things being equal, GNP will remain the same.

If a new product is created, then GNP will be increased by the amount of money spent on this product. By the same token, people will have to divert an equal amount of money from other goods and services in order to buy the new product; thus GNP for all other goods and services will fall by an equal amount. The increase in GNP from the new product will just cancel out the decrease in GNP from all other products, and, other things being equal, total GNP will remain the same.

In other words, of the two possible ways to create wealth, neither of them will result in an increase in GNP.

But, if during the period under question, the banks increase the supply of paper money, then people will spend more for all sorts of things. (They will have more to spend.) Thus GNP will rise whether there is an increase in the real wealth of the country or not. In short, an increase in the real wealth of the country will not, other things being equal, cause an increase in GNP. But an increase in the supply of money will cause an increase in GNP whether there is an increase in real wealth or not.

If you question an economist about this, he will answer that ordinary GNP is an unfortunate statistic which has been seized upon by the public; he relies on what he calls real GNP, which is GNP minus a factor to account for "inflation." I.e., if GNP has risen by 8% and the depreciation of the currency has boosted prices by 5%, then real GNP is said to have advanced by 3%. Real GNP is a better concept than plain GNP, but it is still subject to fallacies. The main fallacy is that our methods of measuring the depreciation of the currency are inaccurate and tend to understate the rate. (What if the rate of depreciation is really 8% and not 5% as measured? Then in the above example the whole increase in real GNP is due to statistical error.)[1] The problem with the Consumer Price Index as a measure of currency depreciation is that it is the only measure in terms of the actual goods people buy and so there is nothing against which to check it. The only time there has been something against which to check the Consumer Price Index was during the Civil War period when gold (which had just been de-monetized) was trading on the free market. The price of gold served as one measure of the depreciation of the paper money, and the Consumer Price Index served as another measure. By 1864, the price of gold was up over 100% in terms of paper money, indi-cating a depreciation of over half, and the Consumer Price Index was up 77%.

Since the Consumer Price Index is an index designed to go up in accord with the depreciation of the currency and GNP is an index which goes up in accord with the depreciation of the currency, it can reasonably be asked: What does one get when one corrects GNP by subtracting the CPI?

Go back to the case of the inventor who develops a cheaper way to produce electric power. There is no rise in GNP from this gain in wealth, but there will be a rise in real GNP. This is because with electric power cheaper the Consumer Price Index will fall; hence real GNP will rise. This is fairly straightforward; however, most inventions and improvements do not simply make the same good cheaper; they introduce improvements in quality. An attempt is made to compensate for this by estimating the value of the im-provement. Suppose the invention consists of an improvement in the quality of sound on one's hi-fi. The bureaucrats who compute the CPI say something like, "This is a 5% improvement in sound quality for the same price; therefore, it is equivalent to a 5% reduction in price for the same quality. Therefore, we treat this as a 5% reduction in price when we compute CPI."

Thus the major real factor which is affecting real GNP is some obscure government official saying, "Well I think that Xerox ma-chines give a better image now than they did last year; let's use that fact to offset the price increase for their product. I think cars are giving a better ride than they did previously," etc.

As Linda Jenness, Socialist Workers Party candidate for Presi-dent in 1972, pointed out in this regard: "Take automobiles, for example. From the introduction of the 1959 models through the 1970 models, car prices increased by hundreds and thousands of dollars in that period. But the Consumer Price Index registered no increases in auto prices!"[2]

In short, when one penetrates all the complex mathematics, what is at the bottom of real GNP is the scientific equivalent of your grandmother saying: "Well it seems to me that life is better now than it was when I was a little girl. People have nicer homes and nicer cars, and they seem to eat better and have more free time." There is nothing wrong, as such, with your grandmother's judgments. The point is that, at best, our modern economist can approach them in accuracy. And of course even real GNP does not do that. If we remember the story of the enterprising farmer, we realize that, during an issue of paper money, in money terms it appears as though everyone has gained. And GNP, of course, is an attempt to measure the economy by translating everything into terms of money. There are three specific factors—side effects of the paper money expansion—which go to increase real GNP while lowering the real wealth of the people in the society:

(1) Inventory accumulation: Almost all businessmen hold inventories. They wish to make these inventories large enough to economize on transportation costs and to be able to satisfy customers' wishes. But they also wish to keep the inventories from getting too large because inventory ties up capital and costs the businessman interest. Each businessman works out his own proper level of inventories in consideration of these factors and the peculiarities of his business.

However, when the process of money creation lowers the rate of interest, it makes sense for the businessman to increase his inventories. This is what happened from 1965 to 1970. The inventory/sales ratio of all manufacturing and trade hit a low of 1.43 in early 1966 and rose to a high of 1.64 in 1970 (First National City Bank of N.Y., "Monthly Economic Letter," Oct. 1971). During this period, workers worked overtime and some of the unemployed were hired in order to overstock the warehouses of the nation. This increased GNP, but it did not create goods for people's use. So long as the goods merely piled up in warehouses they could not be used by people. And the only conditions under which they would be likely to come out of the warehouses (i.e., a reduction in the inventory/sales ratio) are the conditions of a declining GNP.

(2) The Austrian effect: There is another way in which the

country can increase production without increasing the ultimate good to people. This was demonstrated by Murray Rothbard of the Austrian school of economics. It results from the fact that people must always make a choice between consumption and investment. Either use your wealth now, enjoy it and consume it, or invest it and use it to give you more wealth later. Common sense dictates that a reasonable balance must be maintained between consumption and investment. The man who consumes everything is the wastrel, always in debt. The man who invests everything is the miser who never enjoys his wealth. Each person in our society makes a decision on how much of his income he will consume and how much he will invest according to his own preference.

If businessmen see that people are consuming more, they will shift to making more consumer goods—goods that will be used up directly. If businessmen see that people are investing more, they will shift to making more capital goods, machinery and things which cannot be consumed themselves but which will be used to increase production to give a return on the investment.

For example, if John Jones decides to consume his wealth, he may buy a car. In this case he gives his money to General Motors, and they produce a car for him. If he decides to invest his wealth, he may buy a General Motors bond. In this case he has lent his money to GM, and they will use it to build a new factory which, five years from now, will produce cars more efficiently. GM's decision to build cars or to build factories is ultimately related to John Jones' decision to consume or invest.

When the banks create money by making loans, these loans typically are to businessmen who invest in capital goods. This leads to a shift toward investment and away from consumption. From the point of view of society as a whole, it is as if millions of John Joneses had simultaneously decided to consume less and invest more. Several years from now, as the new factories are built, production will rise and real GNP will increase. However, if the John Joneses had wanted to postpone their consumption and get more later, they would have done so; they would have chosen to invest. That they did not indicates that they did not want to. The miser in his old age is very wealthy, but how much has he enjoyed life? If we view wealth as the satisfaction of human desires (which is a more humanistic concept of wealth) rather than merely the production of more widgets, then once again paper money has increased real GNP while decreasing the wealth of the country.

It is this aspect of a paper money expansion of credit which has fooled many economists into defending the system and thinking that it actually does create wealth. Viewing this aspect and this aspect alone, there are more "things" in existence because of the expansion. There are more widgets and automobiles, etc. The effect here is to force the average person to make the investment choice (as per the miser) rather than the consumption choice.

You can see just how beneficial this would be if it were done openly and directly. Suppose the government were to pass a law which forced people to save and invest 50% of their income. This would mean a drastic curtailment of living standards in the present; but there would be an increase in wealth in the future. The question is: Would people be better off from that later increase in view of the hardships they would have to suffer in the present?

I think it is clear that the answer is no. If a person feels that he is better off by saving 50% of his income for the future, then he is free to do so, but very few people make that choice. This open and direct method will likewise increase GNP because, in the future, the capital goods will allow increased production. But it is not to people's economic benefit. If it were, they would make the choice voluntarily.

(3) Waste due to overemotionalism of a boom: In the euphoria which swept over the stock market in 1967-68, it was not only the paper value of stocks which had a boom and bust. The rising value of those stocks led directly to new construction of factories and outlets. Since this new construction was based on artifically high stock prices and not on reality, most of it was waste and was revealed as waste when the stocks collapsed. A most notorious example was the fast food franchising business. Certain unscrupulous operators were using accounting tricks which made their companies appear far more profitable than they really were. One of these tricks was to sell a franchise on time and then count all of the income from the sale (not merely the down payment) as *this year's* earnings (even though the company would not receive all of the money for several years). Once this trick was established, the

idea was to see who could sell the most franchises. But of course, every time a franchise was sold so that this accounting trick could be worked, a real live restaurant was constructed. The country was then flooded with fast food places which could not justify their existence economically; much of the labor and materials which went into building them turned out to be waste. That labor and those materials could have been used far more effectively to benefit people. But they all counted as big pluses in GNP.

In 1968, in this country, there was a mood of economic euphoria. Everyone was talking of millionaires, and celebrities were endorsing quickie franchise operations. But my mood at this time was not euphoric. When I would see a workman constructing a new Lums or a giant office building, I recognized this as waste. What is the fate of a society which sets one group of men to building walls and another group to tearing them down? The labor of those men, the bricks, the plumbing, the wiring and all the materials that went into the building of those restaurants, office buildings and other phony projects were waste. They added to GNP, but they subtracted from the nation's wealth.

It should also be pointed out that, if there are more things in existence from the Austrian effect, this is more than counterbalanced by the waste. The country is thus in the position of being forced to save in order that it may have less in the future.

A point that should be made here is that there is a tragic human consequence of this process. Factors 1, 2 and 3 not only involve the misuse of resources, they involve the misuse of human labor. Put quite simply, a boom creates a demand in the economy for different goods than would be demanded if there had been no boom. When workers are hired to produce these boom-type goods, their jobs are secure only so long as the boom continues. Any diminution in the rate of paper money creation will throw these people out of work. This is why in 1970 there was so much unemployment among scientists. The shift to making more capital, described in factor 2, led to a demand for basic research (which is a capital good) requiring more Ph.D.'s. The high demand for these people led to high salaries for this group several years ago and induced many young men with the requisite intelligence to get advanced degrees and compete for jobs in these fields. But the reduction in the rate of money creation in 1969 coincided with the graduation from school of large numbers of these Ph.D.'s, and since their jobs were dependent on the boom, we had the phenomenon of unemployed Ph.D.'s in 1970. Thus large numbers of the nation's brightest men were induced to spend crucial years of their lives preparing themselves for jobs which were will-o'-the-wisps, mirages, which would not exist in a proper economy.

The solution of the banking elite to this human tragedy was not to prevent such misuse of labor. It was to recreate the jobs by another round of paper money. Thus another generation is being drawn into this cycle, who in turn will become the justification for another round of paper money. This is the solution of the drunkard who combats the bad effects of the hangover by getting drunk again.

To summarize, GNP, like stock prices, corporate profits, housing starts, etc., goes up because of the same process which enriches the bankers and business at the expense of the rest of the community—the printing of paper money. The claim that these common modes of measuring the growth of the economy actually do that is false. What they measure is not the public interest but the interest of the banks and big business. When these latter gain, the great majority of Americans lose. It is a fall in GNP which is to the economic interest of most of the American people.

Myth 2. The myth of altruism.
Surely our age is blessed with the most beneficient leaders. All of them possess the greatest degree of heartfelt concern for the poor and unfortunate souls who cannot find employment. Have we not enacted into law the Employment Act of 1946, which makes it a policy of the government to reduce unemployment? Is this not a prime concern of politicians of both parties, of labor leaders, and have not even businessmen become enlightened to recognize their obligations along this line?

All this is by way of contrast to that evil age of 70 years ago when politicians were unconcerned with unemployment, unions were almost powerless to protect jobs and business leaders could say, "The public be damned."

So no one will be surprised to see the rates of unemployment

ILLUSTRATION 3

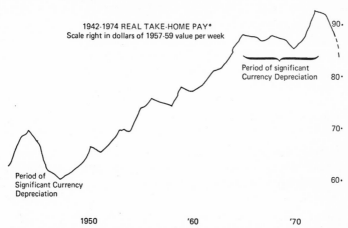

1942-1974 REAL TAKE-HOME PAY*
Scale right in dollars of 1957-59 value per week

Period of significant
Currency Depreciation

Period of
Significant Currency
Depreciation

90·

80·

70·

60·

1950   '60   '70

*Annual spendable average weekly earnings of production or nonsupervisory workers in manufacturing.
This does not include deductions for State and City income taxes and other local deductions from
weekly paychecks. Source, U.S. Bureau of Labor Statistics, "Employment and Earnings Statistics for
the United States 1909-67" Bulletin 1312-5. Worker with three dependents

ILLUSTRATION 4

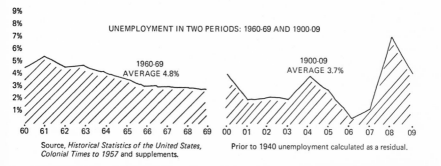

UNEMPLOYMENT IN TWO PERIODS: 1960-69 AND 1900-09

1960-69
AVERAGE 4.8%

1900-09
AVERAGE 3.7%

9%
8%
7%
6%
5%
4%
3%
2%
1%

60 61 62 63 64 65 66 67 68 69   00 01 02 03 04 05 06 07 08 09

Source, *Historical Statistics of the United States,*   Prior to 1940 unemployment calculated as a residual.
Colonial Times to 1957 and supplements.

for our recent history and for 70 years ago. (See Illustration 4 on page 43.)

Average unemployment in the first decade of the century was 3.7% per year. (This figure is from the Bureau of Labor Statistics; the National Industrial Conference Board's "Economic Record" of 3/20/40 estimated it as 3.4%.) Average unemployment in the decade of the '60s was 4.8% per year. The first decade was a time of mild currency depreciation (the price level rose by 10% over the ten years) and a time of a huge influx of foreign labor which underbid American workers for their jobs. The decade of the 1960s was a decade of rampant currency depreciation when foreign labor was kept out by strict immigration laws. By all of the myths which we have been taught, the decade of the 1960s should have been a decade of lower unemployment than the first decade of the century.

An important point to note is that the unemployment rate was more volatile 70 years ago than it is now. It went higher in periods of depression and lower in periods of boom. The unemployment rate of .8% in 1906 is simply unachievable in modern times. The significance of this is that the real hardship of unemployment does not fall on those who are just temporarily between jobs; it falls on the hard-core unemployed—those who remain out of work for long periods of time. It is hard to see how unemployment could have gotten down to .8% in 1906 and 1.8% in 1907 if there were any significant number of hard-core unemployed. This indicates that even the unemployment that did exist at that time was more of the between-jobs type of unemployment and far less of the hard-core type. Permanent, hard-core unemployment is a modern phenomenon, and it arrived on the scene *after* the air became filled with platitudes expressing sympathy for the plight of the unemployed. Perhaps the point of this section can best be made by a story told to me by a friend in the securities business.

My friend worked for the proprietor of a small mutual fund; call him Mr. X. Mr. X's fund had done well in the wild stock market of 1967 and 1968. The policy of paper money expansion followed during those years helped to create an emotionalism which put all kinds of low-priced cats and dogs (low quality, high risk stocks) up far beyond any rational estimate of their value. In the process, Mr. X's low-priced stocks went up, enriching him and drawing many more people into his fund. By the time of my story, he was quite wealthy and also a large contributor to the campaign funds of certain prominent politicians.

But the attempt to stop "inflation" which began in December 1968 (and ultimately had its effect in a significantly lower rate of price increase by early 1971) was not good for Mr. X. It sent the stock market into a tailspin and pulled the support out from under the over-priced cats and dogs. By June of 1969, Mr. X's fund was losing money hand over fist.

Mr. X did not attempt to save his clients' money by selling off stocks and staying out of the market until the decline was over. Instead he wrote a letter to one of the politicians dependent on him for financial support. 'Speak out,' he said 'against the economic policies of the Nixon administration. I am indignant at the terrible suffering which is being caused to the unemployed of this nation. In the name of these people, there must be a return to the policies of 1967-68.'[3]

In contrast to the other myths perpetrated by the banking establishment, it is correct to say that the unemployed are helped by a business boom (i.e., a paper money expansion)—at least in the short run. During periods of boom, the unemployment rate goes down (a little); during periods of recession, it goes up. In short, while the instant millionaires of the late 1960s were wheeling and dealing in their conglomerates, while Howard Levin was ordering his $900 attache case and Bernard Cornfeld was throwing his wild parties, a small percentage of the working force was picking up its $1.60-$1.70/hr., whereas it otherwise would not have been able to do so.

Thus perhaps it would be justified to say that out of all this evil comes a little good. Someone at least benefits from the paper money besides the establishment which brings it about. Unfortunately not even this is the case. This view is valid for the short run but not for the long run. Paper money does reduce the rate of unemployment for a two to five year period, but viewed on a scale of 10 to 20 years, the effect is just the opposite.

Consider the following argument: What if our society succeeded in putting an end to unemployment? What if the percentage of unemployed dropped to the level it had maintained during the first decade of this century, with that level consisting of people who were clearly between jobs and who would be employed again within a few months? What then would the banking establishment use as a reason to promote policies of "stimulation of the economy?" Would they say, "Simulate the economy so that I can make a bundle of money?" No, coming from the mouth of Mr. X and people like him, this argument would fall flat on its face. These people need the unemployed; they need them badly. They need them to mask the self-interest underlying their demands and cloak it in an aura of altruism. If the unemployed did not exist, they would have to create them.

And create them is what they do. For unemployment in our society is not a natural phenomenon. Unemployment is deliberately manufactured by the policies of the aristocracy; it is created in order that they may posture as the friends of the unemployed and, by throwing a few crumbs to these unfortunates, rob billions of dollars from the people of America.

It should be noted that the phenomenon of long term, hardcore unemployment is far worse than is registered by the unemployment rate of 5-6%. When a man cannot find work for too long a time, he may become discouraged and give up—thus dropping out of the labor force so that he is no longer counted in the unemployment statistics. Approximately 15% of the population of New York City is on welfare. How many of these could or would be willing to work if they could find jobs is a matter for conjecture, but to say that the human tragedy of inability to find work is accurately recorded by an unemployment rate of 5-6% is an error.

If all 15% of those on welfare in New York City represent people driven from the labor force by policies of the aristocracy, then the true rate of unemployment for New York City is of the order of magnitude of 20%, which is to say that we have a long term, hard-core unemployment problem as bad as it was during the worst days of the depression. These policies work by the following means:

(1) Labor union unemployment: Some unions, in order to raise wages, limit the number of jobs in their field. They believe (correctly) that if there are fewer workers, the law of supply and

demand will make it easier for them to get high wages. For example, the taxi union in New York City has pressured the Mayor into restricting the number of hack licenses. Many people who otherwise would be employable as taxi drivers in New York therefore remain unemployed. Similarly, construction unions severely limit the number of apprentices they allow. This creates a shortage of skilled construction workers. The Teamsters Union, together with their employers, the trucking companies, pressure the ICC to limit the number of interstate truckers. This forces truckers' fees and teamsters' wages up and keeps the unemployed from finding jobs driving trucks.

It is easy to see why these unions do this; their members want higher wages, and they are perfectly willing to climb up to greater heights of prosperity on the backs of their fellows whom they kick down into the ranks of the unemployed. It is less easy to see why laws are passed allowing them to do these things. The mayor of New York claims to be a liberal and to have sympathy for the unemployed. Why, then, does he not allow them the opportunity to earn their own living? Does one man have the right to forbid another man to work?

Many of these practices have led to serious racial disturbances. The restrictive practices of the New York taxi union seem to be related to color as most of the people who are prevented from obtaining taxi jobs are black. These blacks operate illegal gypsy cabs, earning their living in defiance of the law. The racial animosity engendered by this situation has made it extremely dangerous for white cab drivers to enter the black areas of the city. The restrictive practices of the construction unions are well known, and civil rights groups have made attempts to break the color bar—with little success.

Note that the prime evil is not the action of the unions. They are simply acting in the interests of their members. The prime evil is the legislation which enables them to achieve this benefit by forcing other people into the ranks of the unemployed.

(2) Minimum wage law unemployment: The minimum wage compels employers to pay their workers a minimum of a certain amount (now $2.30/hour[4]). This law has no application to the great majority of workers, who are worth far more than

$2.30/hour and are paid wages well above that amount. However, it does have application to workers who are not worth $2.30/hour to their employers. If a man produces goods worth $2.00 in an hour, his employer will find it profitable to employ him at $1.95/hour, but not at $2.05/hour. Because of the minimum wage law, therefore, his employer has an economic inducement to fire this man (or not to hire him in the first place), to replace him with a machine, if possible, or not to go into an area of business where he will have to hire many of such kinds of people. Such unfortunates fill the ranks of the unemployed. (Unemployment rates for minority youth run in the range of 25-40%.)

It is evident that, if the unemployed were given the choice, they would choose to have the minimum wage abolished. Since they cannot get jobs at $2.30/hour, they would prefer to have a chance to get them at $2.20 or $2.00. At the very worst they could reject these inferior jobs and be in the same situation they are in today. But at least they would have the freedom of choice. How then can such a law be justified as being for the benefit of the poor?

Proponents of the minimum wage argue that without it the wages of the lower level of workers would be driven down to subsistence. But, of course, there is no lower wage than the wage one receives when one is unemployed. The wages of workers worth $3.00/hour are not driven down to $2.00. The wages of workers worth $4.00/hour are not driven down to $3.00. Why should the wages of workers worth $2.00/hour be driven down to $1.00?

Any worker has a bargaining power depending on the value of his labor. If his employer does not want to pay him what he is worth, he can always go to another employer. A worker receiving $3.00/hour who is really worth $4.00/hour will be able to find an employer willing to pay him close to $4.00. This is simply in the self-interest of the employer. The wages of the lower level of workers were not driven down to subsistence prior to the enactment of the minimum wage (Karl Marx, to the contrary, notwithstanding). In fact, wages have increased steadily in this country in terms of real buying power ever since the Pilgrims landed in the Mayflower (with minor setbacks during periods of currency depreciation), and there is no reason to think things would be different now.

The members of the aristocracy who support the minimum wage law do not do so out of sympathy for the lower level of workers. They do so to help create a class of unemployed for whom they can feign sympathy.

Increases in the minimum wage are generally gradual enough so that the unemployment they cause is obscured by other economic factors at the time of the increase. But the initial establishment of the minimum wage in 1938 had an especially marked effect in Puerto Rico because of the large number of workers in that territory worth less than the minimum wage. Unemployment rose so rapidly that in 1940 the Roosevelt administration felt obligated to amend the minimum wage law to make an exception of Puerto Rico. Referring to this amendment, Senor Bolivar Pagan, Resident Commissioner for Puerto Rico said: "It has been said that the application to the islands of the minimum wage rates prescribed by the Fair Labor Standards Act for the mainland of the United States has threatened to cause serious dislocation in some island industries and great curtail of employment. The amendment signed today will permit separate study of this problem and *the fixing of wage rates for these islands* which are high enough to protect industries on the mainland from unfair competition but *which are low enough* to encourage industrial development and to *provide employment opportunities in the islands.* "[5] The Roosevelt administration knew that the measures they offered would throw people out of work. In areas where this caused a significant social problem which would have political implications (such as Puerto Rico), they quietly backed down. But in areas where the unemployed would be scattered and voiceless and have no political power, then no one gave a damn.

Pro-bank economists continue to deny the effect of the minimum wage in throwing the less valuable workers out of work. They admit the operation of the law of supply and demand in other areas. They admit that overpricing of wheat leads to a surplus of unused wheat. But they will not admit that overpricing of labor leads to a surplus of unused labor. These economists cannot approach their subject on the basis of reason. They must defend the myths of the aristocracy which supports them.

ILLUSTRATION 5

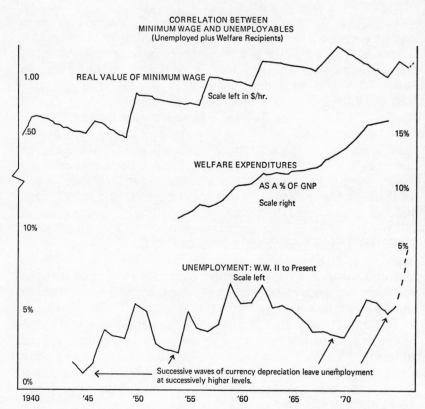

CORRELATION BETWEEN
MINIMUM WAGE AND UNEMPLOYABLES
(Unemployed plus Welfare Recipients)

Sources,
Unemployment: *Historical Statistics of the United States, Colonial Times to 1957* plus supplements.
Welfare: *Statistical Abstract of the United States,* includes Fed. Gov't., most states and some localities.
Real value of the minimum wage is minimum wage divided by CPI (1957-59 = 100).

Since WW II, the minimum wage has gone up, both in real terms and in money terms. Labor unions have become more rigid. The effect is to throw ever larger numbers of people into the ranks of the hard-core unemployed. In this manner, the hard-core unemployed gradually move out of the unemployment statistics and onto the welfare rolls. (Only a small fraction of the total unemployed are unemployed for more than 26 weeks.)

Notice that it is the concept of *unemployment* which gets so much concern, not the concept of *unemployable,* which would include those on welfare who have given up seeking work because they are so discouraged. Even in times of recession, only one-fifth to one-third of the unemployed (that is, 2-3% of the total labor force) represent people who have been unemployed for over 15 weeks. The rest surely represent people who are merely between jobs. The real social tragedy consists of those people who cannot find jobs and so drop out of the labor force (i.e., stop looking for work). Why is our concern not focused on them? The answer to this question is that the unemployment rate is subject to short-term influences. Few people remain on the unemployment rolls for over a year. Thus the *short-term* influences of paper money, which are to reduce unemployment, are clearly reflected in this statistic. But the *long-term* influences of paper money, which are to increase unemployment (in the larger sense), are most clearly shown by looking at the welfare statistics.

The deliberate creation of unemployment in order to justify a policy of paper money has further consequences. A man who has sunk into the ranks of the permanently unemployed suffers a loss, not only of income, but of a part of his diginity. This is a spiritual loss; it can not be measured by the means of economics. But it has a real effect. It is such people who turn to drugs and crime.

There is no social or cultural reason for the large class of welfare dependent people, breeding crime and drug abuse, which has grown up in America during the past generation. Neither is there any genetic or environmental reason. The ancestors of our modern welfare class prior to 1933 were capable of dignity and self sufficiency; they did not turn to drugs and crime. But they had the same cultural milieu, the same genetic background, and, if anything, an even poorer environment.

If a 16-year-old black youth who has dropped out of school is employed for $2.00/hour, then he can earn spending money and contribute to the income of his family. More important, he has a chance to learn some skills and develop habits conducive to work. By the time he is 25, he has a reasonable chance at earning a living. But, if this same boy remains unemployed, then he never receives the training which will make him employable at a higher wage. Rather, he develops the habits of a life of idleness and becomes *less* employable, not more.

In Harlem, there are large numbers of blacks driving gypsy cabs. Their operations are illegal, and white cab drivers do not dare to enter their territory. The establishment has forbidden these men from earning a living. They have the character to fight back, to retain their dignity by breaking the law. These men have experienced the realities of power in America today and know how to evaluate it when phony liberals mouth pretty platitudes to the establishment press about their concern for blacks.

Not everyone has this much character. There are morally weak people in every group; these are the ones who give up, go on welfare and turn to crime and drugs. The black generation of 1865-1900, far more disadvantaged in every way in comparison to our present blacks (except that they lived in a society in which there were no minimum wage laws and in which unions did not have the power to keep people from working), did not do this but were by and large religious people who lived moral lives. These social problems are the consequence of our paper money system, and when that is ended, they will go away.

A few years ago, a British economist named Phillips came up with the idea that there is a trade-off between "inflation" and unemployment. That is, to reduce unemployment we must put up with more "inflation," and to reduce "inflation" we must suffer an increase in unemployment. He even plotted curves showing the amount of "inflation" which is associated with a given amount of unemployment.

Of course the statistics of 70 years ago refute Mr. Phillips' notion. At that time there was very little unemployment with only a mild rise in prices. And since the Phillips curve first became popular among economists, it seems to have shifted. For example, it seemed to require more depreciation of the currency to reduce unemployment to the 4½% level in 1973 than it did to reduce it to the 3½% level in the mid-1960s.

The conventional economists flounder about and pretend they do not know what is happening. But it is very simple. The banker aristocracy, which benefits from paper money, has an interest in creating unemployment. It helps to increase the minimum wage; it helps labor unions to tighten their strangleholds on their various industries. The more unemployment which results from these policies, the more persuasive a case can be made for a further dose of paper money to temporarily reduce the unemployment. Thus structural unemployment is increased, and it requires ever greater rates of currency depreciation to reduce it to the same level.

In addition to serving as the motive for structural unemployment, paper money also causes cyclical unemployment because it leads to the malemployment of human labor as described in the discussion of Myth 1. Paper money distorts the economy so that jobs are created which can only exist as long as the paper money continues. People working in these jobs are malemployed.

For example, when major issues of paper money were issued in 1971 and 1972, it created a boom in the housing industry, and housing starts ran up to a 2.5 million annual rate. Because interest rates had dropped, people found it cheaper to get mortgages and so did more building. When the rate of money expansion was reduced in 1973 and 1974, interest rates rose and housing starts fell below a one million annual rate. Thus many people in the construction field were thrown out of work. They were unemployed in 1974 because they had been malemployed in 1972.

It is true that the paper money issued in 1975 will cause these people to be reemployed. But they will not be properly employed; they will be malemployed in artificial jobs. When the politicians decide it is time to fight "inflation" again, these people will be thrown out of work. They face a lifetime alternating between "inflation" and unemployment.

The Loco-Foco movement (a left-wing splinter of the Democratic Party which appeared in the 1830s and advocated an end to all bank issues of paper money in excess of their gold and silver) used to say in explanation of this dilemma: When the currency expands, the loaf contracts; when the currency contracts, the loaf disappears. That is, when more paper money is issued, the worker is cheated by the fall in his real wages; when the paper money is restricted, the artificial jobs cease to exist, and he is unemployed.

When faced with the problem of cyclical unemployment, the proper course of action is to allow the unemployed workers to find real jobs, not to create artificial jobs by new issues of paper money. That will not feed the unearned profits of the bankers, but in the long run it is best for the working man.

Myth 3. The myth of something for nothing.

In Chapter III, we discussed economists who believed that paper money was the magic road to wealth, that it enabled society to create something for nothing. This theory began when paper money first started, in the late 17th century, and some of its infamous practitioners are William Paterson (previously mentioned founder of the Bank of England), John Law (originator of the Mississippi bubble in France) and Dan Shays.

With the development of economic science in the late 18th century, these ideas were rejected and the United States entered a long period of relatively sound money. However, early in the 20th century the something-for-nothing ideas were reestablished, chiefly due to the work of John M. Keynes.

What Keynes did was to take the old mercantilist economic viewpoint, dress it up in modern language and present it as the latest scientific word in economics. Much of Keynesian economics has already been discredited. For example, no one today believes—as Keynes argued—that by breaking a window one increases society's wealth. (Not only was this believed in the 1930s, but in the middle of the depression, the Roosevelt administration adopted a deliberate program of killing hogs in the belief that this would increase the nation's wealth.) However, there is one aspect of Keynesianism which still survives and is widely accepted. Keynes introduced a new argument to prove that paper money creates something out of nothing. What he said was the following:

(1) There exists a portion of the working force which is normally unemployed. These are not merely people who are in a transitional period between jobs. They are people who are actively

seeking work and cannot find it.

(2) Paper money reduces unemployment. (Actually Keynes would have said that government deficit spending reduces unemployment. But government deficit spending would not reduce unemployment if the deficits were not financed through paper money. If government deficits had to be financed by borrowing from the people, then the extra money spent by the government would be exactly counterbalanced by the lesser amount of money spent by those who had lent to it.) As we have seen in the previous sections, the effect of a depreciation of the currency is to lower the workingman's real wages. When all is said and done, this is how paper money reduces unemployment. Paper money leads to a depreciation of the currency; this lowers the real value of wages. Employers see that wages are lower and thus find it expedient to hire more workers.

Paradoxically, it is just when wages are suffering the most that public opinion thinks that they are going up. When prices are rising and workingmen demand a wage boost to keep pace with the cost of living, the newspapers scream headlines about the demands of the greedy unions. Conversely, in a depression, when the real value of wages is going up (because prices drop more rapidly than wages) but money wages are going down, the public is filled with sympathy for the worker. The public is fooled by money wages and does not look at real wages.

(3) Since some of the unemployed are now working, more goods are being produced.

(4) Conclusion: Paper money has created something out of nothing.

Jefferson commented on this point of view almost 160 years ago:

> Like a dropsical man calling out for water, water, our deluded citizens are clamoring for more banks, more banks. The American mind is now in that state of fever which the world has so often seen in the history of other nations. We are under the bank bubble, as England was under the South Sea bubble, France under the Mississippi bubble, and as every nation is liable to be under whatever bubble, design, or delusion may puff up in moments when off their guard. We are now taught to believe that

legerdemain tricks upon paper can produce as solid wealth as hard labor in the earth. It is vain for common sense to urge that *nothing* can produce but *nothing;* that it is an idle dream to believe in a philosopher's stone which is to turn everything into gold, and to redeem man from the original sentence of his Maker, "in the sweat of his brow shall he eat his bread."[6]

Keynes indeed did teach that legerdemain tricks upon paper (manipulation of the Federal budget) can produce solid wealth. If this process works, it is certainly a wonderful thing. If we can create something out of nothing, then we should surely do it. Why not print up billions and billions of paper dollars until there is no unemployment at all? This would give us the maximum effect of something for nothing and would fill the humanitarian goal of ending unemployment.

In fact, Keynes argued that when paper money was used in this way, it would not lead to a depreciation of the currency (i.e., a rise in prices). He claimed that, since more goods are being produced, this balances off the fact that there is more money in existence; therefore, a given amount of money will still buy the same quantity of goods.

The Keynesians thus believe that, as long as there is unemployment in the society, you can safely issue paper money without causing "inflation." If there is unemployment, you have not issued enough paper money. If there is "inflation," you have issued too much. According to this theory there can not be both unemployment and "inflation" at the same time. But there is, in America today, both unemployment and "inflation." There has been both unemployment and "inflation" for most of the last 42 years.

In the summer of 1971, Arthur Burns, the Chairman of the Federal Reserve Board, said, "The old laws of economics aren't working like they used to." Mr. Burns was disturbed by the existence of a 6% rate of unemployment together with substantial "inflation." The "old laws" to which he was refering were the "laws" of Keynesian economics, to which Mr. Burns subscribes.

The error in the Keynes argument is in Step 1. This step appears plausible because there is, in fact, unemployment in our society. But as we have seen in the previous section, this unemployment is caused by artificial government acts which prevent people from working. Take away these artificial government restrictions on employment, and aside from the minimal amount of unemployment which is due to people who are temporarily between jobs, unemployment in our society would be zero.

Every person's labor has a value. That value consists of the value of the goods he is capable of producing. It is always profitable for an employer to hire a worker for less than the value of his labor. It is never profitable for an employer to hire a worker for more than the value of his labor. Most people are hired for approximately the value of their labor.

If someone is unemployed, the reason is that he is asking more for his labor than any employer thinks he is worth. It may be painful to a man's self concept, but what he must do is to lower his demands. Then he can find employment.

It stands to reason that there will always be some people who ask more than they are worth and some people who never quite succeed in persuading employers to give them what they are worth or who have a hard time finding their exact niche. But these people will not represent *permanent* unemployment. The man will have to lower his wage demands or search a little harder; but it is scarcely credible that he will sit like a dummy and not do what is required to find work.

This is the reason that unemployment rises rapidly in a period of declining prices (appreciation of the dollar). If a man's salary is $10,000 and if prices in that society then decline in half, then the dollar has appreciated to twice its value; his $10,000 in wages is really worth $20,000. In such circumstances it is not a surprise that his employer fires him. The employer cannot afford to pay him so much. This man may not want to believe that in terms of the new, appreciated currency his salary ought to be $5,000. He may spend a long time looking for a new job at his old salary. It does not occur to him that, because of the appreciation of the currency, a salary of $5,000 would be equivalent to his old salary of $10,000. Thus he continues to turn down job offers which he thinks are beneath him. This phenomenon was responsible for much of the unemployment during the depression.

If you take the Keynesian viewpoint and think what it means in personal terms, then what Keynes was saying was that a man would choose to remain unemployed permanently rather than adjust his wage demands to a realistic level that would get him a job. This is absurd on the face of it. Some people may be slow in adjusting their wage demands. Some people may hold unreasonable expectations. But to say that people will simply sit, like blocks of wood, with unreasonable wage demands for ever and ever does not correspond to the actions of real people in the real world.

This is why the Keynesian theory on "inflation" and unemployment does not work. The unemployed in our society are not those who sit with unreasonable wage demands. They are those who are made unemployable by the minimum wage and by restrictive labor union practices and those who have been malemployed.

It is true that a currency depreciation will temporarily reduce unemployment. The reason for this is that the excess profits of business are so big that there is competition to expand, and this spurs the demand for workers (such as the demand for scientists previously described). It is as though you allow a man to rob you throughout the week because you get a little bit of the money back by working for him on Saturday. But in viewing this as an argument for paper money, the following must be kept in mind:

(1) The reduction in unemployment is temporary. As we have seen, over the long term there is a tendency for unemployment to rise under paper money.

(2) The greatest unemployment occurs in a depression when prices are declining. The reason for this is, as we have seen above, that people are slow to adjust their wage demands to the rise in value of the dollar. But of course the principal reason for a depression is the boom which preceeded it. That is, during the boom the banks issued paper money until they were overexpanded and were forced to contract. The contraction caused a decline in prices with resulting unemployment.

It is therefore not valid to argue for paper money expansion as a cure for unemployment. The contraction is the result of the previous expansion. Had there been no paper money expansion, there would be no contraction and no unemployment.

(3) The ideal state is a condition where there is no expansion of paper money and no contraction. If we had such an economy and

there were no minimum wage law and the labor unions could not use their coercive power to reduce employment opportunities in their fields, then there would be effectively no unemployment. That is, the only unemployed would be those people who are between jobs and whose period of unemployment lasts only a few weeks or a couple of months.

At the end of WW II there occurred what was almost a laboratory test of Keynesian economics. Keynesians believe that the number of employers in a society is, relatively speaking, a fixed quantity. They do not understand that many employers will spring up if wages are low, and few will appear if wages are high. They did not recognize that the large scale unemployment of the Depression was caused by high real wages. They thought it was a feature of the American economy. Their explanation for the low unemployment in the early '40s was that the war had siphoned off 10,000,000 men from the labor force. When these 10,000,000 ex-servicemen hit the civilian economy, they predicted, unemployment would rise to the neighborhood of 10,000,000. We would be back in the Depression.

However, what happened was that during WW II there had been a severe depreciation of the currency. Prices had risen sharply from their 1940 levels. This had the effect of reducing real wages. Thus when the servicemen returned to work in 1946 and 1947, they found it easy to get jobs.

When the unemployment did not appear, the Keynesian economists looked around for an excuse. They found it in the concept of consumer demand. No one can measure consumer demand and no one can define too precisely what it is. Therefore, no one can ever know whether it is present in greater or lesser quantities. When a Keynesian economist is wrong in his predictions, he does not question his theories; he merely postulates a quantity of consumer demand sufficient to explain the difference between his prediction and reality. He then explains that he was unable to read the mind of the consumer. This is a pretty explanation. It means that his theories never have to face the test of reality. If his predictions are right, well and good. If they are wrong, postulate a consumer demand. This procedure flies in the face both of scientific method and common sense. A theory which cannot be put to any test against reality cannot claim the status of a truth.

FOOTNOTES

[1] See Raymond F. DeVoe's article "Statistics Don't Lie" in the July 5, 1971 issue of *Barron's.*

[2] Linda Jenness, "A Program to Combat Soaring Prices " *Inflation, What Causes It, How to Fight It* (New York, 1973), pp. 18-19.

[3] I use single quotes here to indicate that this is not a direct quotation; merely, the substance is accurate.

[4] Effective Jan. 1, 1976.

[5] Senor Bolivar Pagan, as quoted in *Puerto Rico Labor News* (Dept. of Labor, Gov't of Puerto Rico, May-August 1940), III, Nos. 3-4, p. 76, My italics.

[6] Thomas Jefferson, letter to Colonel Charles Yancy, Jan. 6, 1816, *Writings,* XIV, p. 381, Jefferson's italics.

CHAPTER V

The Modern Priesthood

In backward societies there usually exists a relationship between the political leaders and the intellectuals similar to that described by Ayn Rand in her categorization of Attila and the Witch Doctor. The political leader gives the intellectual a comfortable, prestigious perch in the society (an ample income and freedom from material concerns). And the intellectual convinces the average person to accept the rule of the political leader.

This symbiotic relationship arises from the nature of an aristocracy. In order to make exploitation worthwhile, the exploiting class must be much smaller than the exploited. If 70% of the people enslave the other 30%, they can not get enough from them to make it worthwhile. But if 5% of the people can enslave the other 95%, then they can live in luxury off the labor of others.

The problem is that 5% of the population cannot enslave 95% by pure force. The power is clearly on the side of the majority. What is the solution to this? The solution, as practiced countless times throughout history, lies with the intellectuals. The function of the intellectual in this context is to convince the 95% majority that the system which exploits them is proper and just (or necessary and unavoidable or eternal and true). In the Middle Ages the priests preached submission to the kings and nobles and told the people that a bad ruler was the punishment of God. Rebellion was disobedience to God.

For convincing the vast majority to submit to their own exploitation, the intellectual is rewarded by the aristocracy with money and prestige. From the original witch doctor to the Medieval priest to the Communist theoretician of today, most intellectuals have played this role. The shining exceptions were the intellectuals of the 17th and 18th centuries (such as Locke and Jefferson) who preached freedom for the people and resistance to aristocracies.

In the 20th century we have seen a return to the Medieval type of intellectual, but now he is not garbed in the robe of a priest. Now he adopts a modern point of view and dresses himself in the guise of science. No longer does he talk of ethics and theology; in tune with the times, he talks of economics. But his function is the same as that of the Medieval priest—to rationalize and justify the current aristocracy and convince the majority of people to submit to it.

Modern economics claims to be a science. This is a sham and a fraud. It has all of the outer paraphernalia of science and none of its essence. It ostentatiously flaunts mathematical symbols (such as the supply and demand functions) and formulae (MV=PT) without any real understanding of what these things are. When it fails to predict future events (an occurrence of continual embarrassment to modern economists), it does not act like the scientist, disregarding false theories in search of the truth; it acts like the Indian Medicine Man who has failed to make rain. It equivocates, rationalizes and tries to make minor adjustments.

This is because modern economics can not disregard its theories. It must cling to its present theories because it is these theories which rationalize and justify the present aristocracy. And it is by virtue of supporting the aristocracy that modern economists get their prestigious positions in business, government and universities. Modern economists are like the priests of the Middle Ages. They have created a set of myths to convince the majority of Americans to acquiesce in their own exploitation.

What really happens in the world is that there are two groups of people; one has the privilege of creating paper money and the other has the obligation to accept it. The first group uses its privilege to exploit the second. When this exploitation occurs, the economists label the phenomenon a boom and claim that everyone is gaining. When the exploitation slows, they label it a recession. When the exploitation goes into reverse and the common people regain some of their losses, they call it a depression.

The gains on the part of business and the banks are called "stimulation of the economy." The losses on the part of the common person are called "inflation." In this way modern economics pretends that these are two different phenomena, and the objective they preach is to have the first without the second.

But these are not different phenomena. They are part and parcel of the same phenomenon. If a bank can print paper money and get richer by it, then you and all of the other people are getting poorer. There is no way to have "stimulation of the economy" without "inflation." If a thief steals my money, you can not applaud his gain and deplore my loss and resolve to try to have one without the other. His gain *is* my loss.

Yet it is precisely the attempt to "stimulate the economy" without causing "inflation" which constitutes the economic policy of every country in the "free" world. As we have seen, according to the Keynesian mythology "stimulation of the economy" (i.e., issuing paper money) will not cause "inflation" (i.e., depreciation of the currency) as long as there is unemployment. Of course there is "inflation" on a worldwide scale. But the fact that modern economic theories have never worked at any time in any country does not prevent modern economists from clinging tenaciously to them.

A little perspective can be attained on modern economics by reviewing the state of economic knowledge 150-200 years ago. Milton Friedman has made quite a splash in modern economics with his advocacy of the quantity theory of money. But this "latest word" in today's economic realm was well known in 1810. In that year an American pamphleteer wrote: ". . . there is nothing more evident than that the prices of every article in life is determined by the quantity of money in circulation. . . . Since, then, it has been proved, that increasing the circulation, must necessarily increase the prices of commodities, it becomes evident, that bank notes, by which the money circulation of this country has been so prodigiously increased, are the real cause of the present exorbitant prices of provisions; ... consequently, increasing the quantity of money in one part of society, must have the same effect, as taking so much from the other part. ... Therefore, the bankers might, with as much justice, take a certain sum of money out of their neighbors' pockets, as to increase their own by means of bank notes."[1] And a committee of the British House of Commons reported:

> Your Committee conceive that it would be superfluous to point out in detail, the disadvantages which must result to the country, from any such general excess of currency as lowers its relative value. The effect of such an augmentation of prices upon all money transactions for time; the unavoidable injury suffered by annuitants, and by creditors of every description, both private and public; the unintended advantage gained by government and all other debtors; are consequences too obvious to require proof, and too repugnant to justice to be left without remedy. By far the most important portion of this effect it appears to your Committee to be that which is communicated to the wages of common country labor, the rate of which, it is well known, adapts itself more slowly to the changes which happen in the value of money, than the price of any other species of labor or commodity.[2]

That which was well known to the House of Commons in 1810 is unknown to modern economists. Because, if they had to admit that a depreciation of the currency lowers the wages of the common laborer, they could no longer posture as the friend of the little man. They could no longer rationalize the printing of paper money and they would be of no use to the new aristocratic class.

It is not that such a fact is denied. Keynes himself admitted it. It is simply met by a conspiracy of silence. In the light of all the manufactured "injustices" and all the "oppressed" groups which are extant in our political life today, this very real injustice affecting so great a number of people is never even a subject for discussion. Dissent is tolerated within the bounds the aristocracy finds permissible (Milton Friedman being the radical extreme); but there is no dissent which questions the validity of the system.

A key element in the modern economist's intellectual repertoire is what I call banker language. This is a special terminology designed to rationalize most of the aspects of paper money. If you don't call it a spade, perhaps people can be fooled into thinking it's not a spade:

(1) Reserves—When the original depositors brought their gold to the goldsmith, the moral-legal relationship was quite clear. The gold belonged to the depositor; the goldsmith-banker merely stored it and issued a paper receipt as proof of ownership. If the banker used the depositor's gold for some other purpose, he was a thief. If he issued notes for which there was no gold, he was guilty of fraud.

But bankers began to refer to *their depositor's* gold as *their* reserves. The clear implication was that a banker could do as he liked with *his* reserves. It became "responsible" banking practice to maintain enough reserves so that under ordinary circumstances he could meet all demands for redemption that would be made. For example, a banker might keep 20% reserves. This means that he would issue five times as many bank notes as he had gold. But if it were rare for the public to demand redemption of more than 10% at a time (before new deposits came in to offset the outflow), this was considered "responsible" banking practice.

An analagous situation would be the following: Assume that all men's hats were the same, and in a given hotel there were continual functions so that day in and day out there were always hats deposited with the hat check girl. (The hat check girl issued little tickets which served as receipts so that the men could claim their hats when they wanted them.) Suppose then, that the hat check girl noticed that it was very rare for a demand to come in for more than 50% of the hats at one time without this being offset by a new deposit of hats from new customers. Suppose further that an "enterprising" hat check girl decided to sell 25% of the hats and pocket the money or—what amounts to the same thing—issue tickets for hats which don't exist and exchange those tickets for money. Such an event would clearly be fraudulent. The customers, who have a right to their hats, are being deceived. If the girl maintained that she was doing nothing wrong because the hats were her reserves and she maintained enough "reserves" to meet the normal demand for hats, this argument would not be valid. It is not valid with regard to bankers either.

(2) Paper dollars—As previously noted, the word "dollar" was defined to mean a weight of gold—25.8 grains, 9/10 fine. The paper notes which circulated prior to 1933 were *receipts for dollars.* But in banker language these receipts became dollars. This eased the transition in 1933 when people were forced to accept paper money in place of gold.

(3) Convertibility—When a depositor would take his paper receipt and demand his gold, the bankers called this *converting* paper money into gold. The implication was that paper money and gold money are two kinds of money of equal status and one is being converted into the other. But of course this is not true. The paper bank note was not a kind of money which was converted into gold. It was a receipt which was being *redeemed.* When you take your ticket to the hat check girl and demand your hat, you are not converting the ticket into a hat; similarly, when you take your claim check to the baggage department to claim your baggage, you are not converting your claim check into baggage. The ticket or the claim check is simply a token of the department's promise that the hat or baggage in its possession is yours, and it will give it back to you whenever you demand it.

(4) Balance of payments problem—When too many people come to the bank demanding their gold and the bank begins to get worried that it will have to default on its obligation, this is called a bank run. Between 1944 and 1971, the U.S. central bank allowed foreigners to redeem their notes in gold, but American citizens were not so allowed. When, due to the depreciation of the U.S. currency and the resulting higher prices of U.S. goods, Americans began to buy more from other countries, foreigners began to accumulate more and more central bank notes, some of which were redeemed for gold.

By mid-1971 this had developed into a run on the central bank and led to the August 15, 1971, "gold embargo." But the public was told during this period that the nation had a balance of payments problem.

What is wrong with this is that it is not the *nation's* problem at all. It is the central bank's problem. The event which is threatened by a bank run is that the bank will be forced to stop issuing paper money. This is a problem for the bank and the business interests which benefit from paper money, but it is not a problem for the majority of the people. It is to the benefit of the majority to force the central bank to stop issuing paper money. By saying that the nation has a balance of payments problem economists lead people to believe that a run on the central bank is a threat to their interests.

The developing American aristocracy is based on certain unique principles which distinguish it from traditional aristocracies. America as a nation is still too much a product of the Age of Reason, still too dedicated to the ideal "all men are created equal" to easily accept an aristocratic class. This gives our aristocracy certain problems which no other aristocracy has had.

One of the central pillars of its power is the modern division between liberal and conservative. Both extreme left and extreme right in America have strong anti-aristocratic convictions. Were either of these powerful groups to take control of the government, our aristocracy would be smashed within a few years. The aristocracy maintains its position by continually *balancing* these two large forces and portraying itself as moderate and centrist.

Both left and right in America are descendants of the Jeffersonian tradition, and in the realm of money both have part of the truth. The left retains the anti-bank, anti-big business, pro-democratic elements of Jeffersonianism. The right retains the pro-hard money, balanced budget, small government, laissez-faire elements of Jeffersonianism. What neither left nor right recognizes is that these two sets of views are logically related and parts of a larger whole.

The reason Jefferson was opposed to banks was that banks issued paper money. The reason Jefferson wanted a balanced budget was because budget deficits are traditionally financed through paper money issued by a central bank. The reason Jefferson was anti-big business and pro-the common man was that paper money robs the common man to give to the rich. The reason Jefferson was opposed to large government projects and excessive government spending was that this leads to deficits and thus paper money.

The left in America rages against the wealthy capitalists in the "power structure." The right rages against the "Eastern Establishment" and the "Council on Foreign Relations." Yet both believe that this establishment represents a middle of the road point of view, preferable to the other extreme.

Thus in 1964, when the right made its bid with the Goldwater candidacy, it was defeated by a combination of the center and the left. Similarly in 1972, when the left made its bid with the McGovern candidacy, it was defeated by a combination of the center and the right. Left and right continually find themselves paralyzed and blocked by each other.

But in truth, if left and right would take a closer look at each other's ideas, they would find that they have more in common than they think. The ideas which each espouse were originally part of the Jeffersonian philosophy. It was Jefferson who had an integrated philosophy; it is the modern American left and right which are in contradiction.

The right wants to see a balanced budget, but it is continually raising the alarm of a Communist threat, and it has been a supporter of our two past wars. But wars and armaments have always been financed through paper money. There is no surer way to create budget deficits than to whip up public sentiment against "the enemy." There is no such thing as a sound currency during a war.

The left wants to see a redistribution of wealth from the rich to the poor. But it espouses the Keynesian economic theory which is a rationalization for paper money and which leads to a redistribution of wealth from the poor to the rich. If the left really wants to redistribute the wealth from the rich to the poor, they would be best advised to support an ultra-conservative who would give us a balanced budget.

Perhaps it is a cliche, but in this case it is true. The method of political action to fight the aristocracy must be based on tolerance and good will. The present established order triumphs by a policy of divide and conquer. It feeds on hate. It grows stronger every time liberal and conservative battle. Hate distorts man's reason and

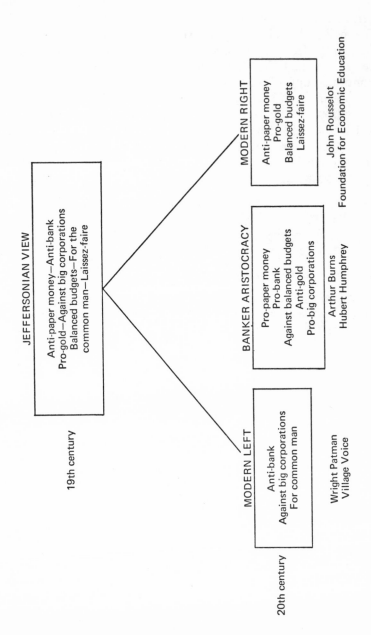

JEFFERSONIAN VIEW

Anti-paper money—Anti-bank
Pro-gold—Against big corporations
Balanced budgets—For the
common man—Laissez-faire

19th century

MODERN LEFT

Anti-bank
Against big corporations
For common man

20th century

Wright Patman
Village Voice

BANKER ARISTOCRACY

Pro-paper money
Pro-bank
Against balanced budgets
Anti-gold
Pro-big corporations

Arthur Burns
Hubert Humphrey

MODERN RIGHT

Anti-paper money
Pro-gold
Balanced budgets
Laissez-faire

John Rousselot
Foundation for Economic Education

prevents each side from seeing where the true enemy lies.

The real political forces in America are those of liberal and conservative. The banker aristocracy is a relatively small political power which maintains its supremacy by keeping these large forces in continual opposition. Both the American left and right have more to gain from the victory of the other than they have from a continuation of the status quo. The Jeffersonian viewpoint is a logical whole, and it is impossible to put one half of it into effect without the other. The first error in modern political thought is when they teach you: "The political arena is divided into liberals and conservatives."

FOOTNOTES

[1] Benjamin Davies, *The Bank Torpedo,* (New York, 1810), p. 7.

[2] "The Bullion Report of the House of Commons, June 8, 1810," as quoted by William G. Sumner, *History of American Currency* (New York, 1968), pp. 387-88.

CHAPTER VI

The Legal Aspect

> Most unquestionably there is no legal tender and there can be no legal tender in this country, under the authority of this government or any other, but gold and silver, either the coinage of our mints or foreign coin at rates regulated by Congress. This is a constitutional principle perfectly plain and of the very highest importance. The States are prohibited from making anything but gold and silver a tender in payment of debts, and although no such express prohibition is applied to Congress, *yet as Congress has no power granted to it in this respect but to coin money and regulate the value of foreign coin,* it clearly has no power to substitute paper or anything else for coin as a tender in payment of debts and in discharge of contracts. (Daniel Webster)[1]

The political revolutions of the 17th and 18th centuries were anti-aristocratic in nature, most especially so the American Revolution. In this tradition the U.S. Constitution was written to prohibit paper money.

It is a comment on the slavish mentality of our age that it cannot grasp this achievement of the 18th century. Americans today do not understand their Constitution. Indeed our present aristocracy could not exist if the Constitution were understood and respected.

This is a crucial point. Operating, as it does, through the power of the government, the banker aristocracy seeks for its dictums the authority of law. What they count on is the respect for law which inheres in most people. This is one of the ways in which 5% of the population can rule the other 95%. The 95% submit to exploitation because they believe it is the law.

Acts establishing paper money certainly appear to be law. They have been enacted by the Congress in accordance with the conventional procedure. People obey them as law. What you must consider at this point are the questions: What is law? Where does *legitimate* authority come from? To what do we morally owe obedience? And, are the legal tender enactments really law?

When the first attempt to make paper a legal tender was made during the Civil War, the Supreme Court struck it down by a vote of five to three. (The court was then composed of eight members.) All three of the votes for constitutionality were appointees of President Lincoln, who had instituted the paper money. But even Lincoln's former Secretary of the Treasury, who had issued the paper money and was then Chief Justice of the Supreme Court, could not support the constitutionality of the legal tender acts.

The paper money advocates, however, were not to be stopped— even by a Supreme Court ruling. One of the five judges who had opposed paper money resigned due to old age, and Congress increased the size of the court from eight to nine, thus giving President Grant two appointees. One of his appointees was a judge who, on a lower court, had ruled paper money constitutional. The other was a corporation lawyer closely associated with the railroad interests. The railroads, carrying large debt loads, were strongly in favor of paper money, and it was widely assumed that this lawyer would represent the interests of his former employers.

Although the court had already declared paper money unconstitutional, the new majority moved to reconsider the issue, and in two cases grouped together under the heading: Legal Tender Cases (*Knox v. Lee* and *Parker v. Davis,* 12 Wall 457) it reversed its former ruling five to four with the two new appointees joining the minority of the previous decision to form the new majority. The

N.Y. World commented: "The decision provokes the indignant contempt of thinking men. It is generally regarded not as the solemn adjudication of an upright and impartial tribunal, but as a base compliance with executive instructions by creatures of the President placed upon the Bench to carry out his instructions."[2]

These historical circumstances present us with some sobering facts. The Republican administrations of Lincoln and Grant had a vested interest in legitimizing the paper money Lincoln had issued during the Civil War. They simply appointed enough Supreme Court justices until they got a ruling in their favor. Of the justices who had been on the bench prior to the enactment of the legal tender acts not one thought them constitutional. It took six appointments to get five votes because Samuel Chase—a man noted for his integrity—refused to subordinate his conscience to the interests of his political party. Clearly no impartial sources believed legal tender acts to be legitimate law. We must now consider the question, from where does legitimate authority come?

There are two doctrines which have been offered to establish the legitimacy of acts of government: The doctrine of divine right of kings and the doctrine of the rights of man. The doctrine of divine right of kings says that God gives all power to the head of the government and that therefore the head of the government has the right to do what he likes with his subjects' lives, liberties and property. In this concept the government is all powerful. Obedience to the government is obedience to God. The common person has no rights whatsoever. Government is unlimited.

The doctrine of the rights of man says that man is born with unalienable rights. Government has no power to violate these rights. The only powers government has are the powers given it by the people.

Most countries in ancient history derived the authority of their government from the doctrine of divine right of kings. In many cases the king was held to actually be a god. America was the first country to be explicitly founded on the doctrine of the rights of man. As the Declaration of Independence states: "We hold these truths to be self-evident—that all men are created equal; that they are endowed by their creator with certain unalienable rights; that among these are life, liberty, and the pursuit of happiness." If people have unalienable rights, then the question arises: How does government get the power to boss them around, to tax them, to regulate them, to establish laws over them? This is the question of legitimate authority. To this question the Founding Fathers of America had an unequivocal answer: In the words of the Revolutionary writer James Wilson: ". . . the only reason why a free and independent man was bound by human laws was this—that he bound himself."[3] In the words of John Adams: "The body politic is formed by a voluntary association of individuals; it is a social compact by which the whole people covenants with each citizen and each citizen with the whole people."[4] As the Declaration of Independence itself concluded: ". . . That, to secure these rights, governments are instituted among men deriving their just powers from the consent of the governed;" The phrase "consent of the governed" has sometimes been interpreted to mean consent of the *majority* of the governed. This was not intended by the Founding Fathers and has no basis in logic. If man has unalienable rights, then the majority can give away their own rights, but they cannot give away the rights of those who disagree with them. The statements of Wilson and Adams make this clear. Freedom of speech, for example, is guaranteed to everyone; even if the majority does not want someone to speak, they have no right to prevent him.

The requirement that government have the voluntary consent of each citizen raises an immediate practical problem. No political association could function if it needed unanimous agreement on every issue. The solution is for the citizens to create a social compact which gives certain general powers to the government and to which the citizen gives his consent.

For example, the citizen may give the government the general power to tax. A citizen may object to a particular tax, but he can not complain that his rights have been violated; he has given the power to tax in general knowing that he will not agree with each use of the power. If he feels that powers are being abused or not being used wisely, he can withdraw his consent, give up his citizenship, and return to a state of nature.

Thus the Founding Fathers felt the need for a document which would be a social compact giving specific powers to a government and winning the consent of the citizens. Such a document was the

U.S. Constitution. This is why America, operating under the doctrine of the rights of man, was the first country to have a constitution. A constitution resolves the problem of legitimate authority.

This point was made by an unknown patriot writing at the time of the Revolutionary War:

> It is easy to perceive that individuals by agreeing to erect forms of government, (for the better security of themselves) must give up some part of their liberty for that purpose; and it is the particular business of a Constitution to mark out *how much* they shall give up. In this sense it is easy to see that the English have no Constitution, because they have given up everything; their legislative power being unlimited without either condition or controul, except in the single instance of trial by Juries. No country can be called *free* which is governed by an absolute power; and it matters not whether it be an absolute royal power or an absolute legislative power, as the consequences will be the same to the people. That England is governed by the latter, no man can deny, there being, as is said before no Constitution in that country which says to the legislative powers, "Thus far shalt thou go, and no farther." There is nothing to prevent them passing a law which shall exempt themselves from the payment of taxes, or which shall give the house of commons power to sit for life, or fill up the vacancies by appointing others, like the Corporation of Philadelphia. In short an act of parliament, to use a court phrase, can do any thing but make a man a woman.
>
> A Constitution, when completed, resolves the two following questions: First, What shall the form of government be? And secondly, what shall be its power? And the last of these two is far more material than the first.[5]

There is a particular result of this which bears directly on the question of the legitimacy of legal tender. This is that the powers of our government are strictly limited to those given in the Constituition. When the government tries to act outside of these powers, it has no legitimate authority. This is the point Daniel Webster was making when he said: "The people, sir, erected this government. They gave it a Constitution, and in that Constitution they have enumerated the powers which they have bestowed on it. They have made it a limited government. They have defined its authority."[6]

This being the case, it should be easy to determine if the legal tender acts are legitimate law. We simply search the Constitution for a grant of such a power. And what do we find? The powers granted to Congress by the Constitution in relation to money are as follows (Art. I, Sect. 8): "To coin Money, regulate the Value thereof, and of foreign Coin, and to fix the Standard of Weights and Measures; . . To provide for the Punishment of counterfeiting the Securities and current Coin of the United States. . . ." No legal tender power was given to the government in the Constitution. This is the meaning of Webster's words above: ". . . as Congress has no power granted to it in this respect but to coin money and regulate the value of foreign coins, it clearly has no power to substitute paper or anything else for coin as a tender in payment of debts and in discharge of contracts."[7] The absence of the legal tender power was not an accident of omission. It was the result of strong feelings on the part of the Founding Fathers about paper money. They made an important distinction between coining money—coining being an operation which referred only to metal—and making paper into money by giving it a legal tender authority. The Constitution was written at a time when the depreciation of the continental (the paper money issued by the Continental Congress to fight the Revolutionary War) was fresh in everyone's mind, and while the Constitutional Convention was making its deliberations, there was a paper depreciation in Rhode Island (See *Federalist* #51). Here are some of the thoughts of the Founding Fathers on the subject:

> . . . a rage for paper money, for an abolition of debts, for an equal division of property, or for any other improper or wicked project, will be less apt to pervade the whole body of the union, than a particular member of it;[8]

> Your surmises relative to a revival of paper currency alarms me. It is impossible that any evil can render such an alternative eligible. It will revive the hopes of the enemy, increase the internal debility of the State, and awaken the clamors of all ranks throughout the United States against her. Much more to Virginia's honor would it be to rescind the taxes, although the consequences of that can but be of a most serious nature.[9]

Here the Legislatures should cooperate with Congress in providing that no money be received or paid at their treasuries, or by any of their officers, or any bank, but on actual weight; in making it criminal, in a high degree, to diminish their own coins, and, in some small degree, to offer them in payment when diminished.[10]

The Constitutional Convention was replete with references to paper money. Here is the general drift of the sentiment:

The great evils complained of were that the State Legislatures run into schemes of paper money &c, whenever solicited by the people, & sometimes without even the sanction of the people (record of June 7, 1787, notes of James Madison on the sentiment of the convention).

Give all power to the many, they will oppress the few. Give all power to the few they will oppress the many. Both therefore ought to have power, that each may defend itself agst. the other. To the want of this check we owe our paper money (June 18, 1787).

The check provided in the 2d. branch was not meant as a check on Legislative usurpations of power, but on the abuse of lawful powers, on the propensity in the 1st branch to legislate too much to run into projects of paper money & similar expedients (July 19, 1787; notes of James Madison on a speech by Gouverneur Morris).

He admitted that inconveniences might spring from the secession of a small number: But he had also known good produced by apprehension of it. He had known a paper emission prevented by that cause in Virginia (August 10, 1787, notes of Madison on a speech by Colonel Mason).

He considered the emissions of paper money (& other kindred measures) as also aggressions (June 19, 1787, Madison is speaking on a plan of Mr. Paterson).

The rights of individuals are infringed by many of the state laws—such as issuing paper money, and instituting a mode to discharge debts differing from the form of the contract (June 19, 1787, notes of Yates on a speech by Madison).[11]

The first draft of the Constitution, as submitted by the committee, permitted states to issue paper money *with the consent of Congress only.* However, this was not good enough for the majority of delegates. Or as reported by one of the delegates, "Mr. Sherman thought this a favorable crisis for crushing paper-money."[12] The prohibition against state-issued paper money was made absolute by a unanimous agreement. This prompted Luther Martin, an advocate of paper money and the abrogation of debts, to declare: "As it was reported by the committee of detail, the States were *only* prohibited from emitting them *without the consent of Congress;* but the convention was so *smitten* with the *paper money dread,* that they insisted that the prohibition be absolute."[13]

Some of the state governments did have the power to issue paper money. Thus to prevent paper money from this source it was necessary for the Federal Constitution to explicitly prohibit the legal tender power to the states; whereas the same end was achieved with regard to the Federal Government merely by not granting any such power. The Constitution states: "No State shall ... coin Money, emit Bills of Credit; make any thing but gold and silver Coin a Tender in payment of Debts;" (Art. I, Sect. 10).

Since the Constitution gives no legal tender power to the Federal Government, we may ask: What did the advocates of paper money use to justify their actions? How could they defend their position? The answer was given by Justice Strong:

> And here it is to be observed it is not indispensable to the existence of any power claimed for the Federal government that it can be found specified in the words of the Constitution or clearly and directly traceable to some one of the specified powers. Its existence may be deduced fairly from more than one of the substantive powers expressly defined or from them all combined. It is allowable to group together any number of them and infer from them all that the power claimed has been conferred. ...
>
> And that important powers were understood by the people who adopted the Constitution to have been created by it, powers not enumerated, and not included incidentally in any one of those enumerated, is shown by the amendments. The first ten of these were suggested in the conventions of the States, and proposed at the first session of the first Congress, before any complaint was made of a disposition to assume doubtful powers. The

preamble to the resolution submitting them for adoption recited that the "conventions of a number of the States had, at the time of their adopting the Constitution, expressed a desire in order to prevent misconstruction or abuse of its powers, that further declaratory and restrictive clauses should be added." This was the origin of the amendments, and they are significant. They tend plainly to show that, in the judgement of those who adopted the Constitution, there were powers created by it, neither expressly specified nor deducible from any one specified power, or ancillary to it alone, but which grew out of the aggregate of powers conferred upon the government, or out of the sovereignty instituted. Most of these amendments are denials of power which had not been expressly granted, and which cannot be said to have been necessary and proper for carrying into execution any other powers. Such, for example, is the prohibition of any laws respecting the establishment of religion, prohibiting the free exercise thereof, or abridging the freedom of speech or of the press.[14]

Justice Strong is arguing that the government has powers not listed in the Constitution. Where did he get such an idea? How can such powers exist without the consent of the governed? From where do they derive their legitimate authority?

Justice Strong was basing his argument on the doctrine of implied powers. This doctrine is thought to derive from Alexander Hamilton; but, as you shall see later, that is an error. The doctrine of implied powers, in the form in which Strong relied on it, was first stated by John Marshall. In a famous Supreme Court decision Marshall had said: "Let the end be legitimate, let it be within the scope of the Constitution, and all means which are appropriate, which are plainly adopted to that end, which are not prohibited, but consistent with the letter and spirit of the Constitution are constitutional."[15]

The trouble with this doctrine is that most of it is so vague as to be meaningless. What are the criteria for legitimacy, appropriateness, being plainly adopted, or being consistent with the spirit of the Constitution? All of these are qualities which will be affirmed by the supporters of every measure and denied by the opponents. The only firm criteria which this doctrine sets forth is that the means should not be prohibited by the Constitution.

This doctrine subtly reverses the entire point of the Constitution. It admits as constitutional anything *not prohibited* by the Constitution. The Founding Fathers intended that nothing would be constitutional except that which was *affirmed* by the Constitution.

Thus we have two entirely different concepts of government. In the one case government has only those powers given to it; in the other government has all powers except those prohibited.

If it be asked how does such a concept of government come into being, where does this government derive its legitimate authority, then we must go back to the doctrine of the divine right of kings. Alexander Hamilton had some interesting things to say on this subject during the debate over a bill of rights. Hamilton opposed writing a bill of rights into the Constitution—but not for the obvious reason:

> It has been several times truly remarked, that bills of rights are, in their origin, stipulations between kings and their subjects, *abridgments of prerogative in favor of privilege, reservations of rights not surrendered to the prince.* Such was MAGNA CHARTA, obtained by the Barons, sword in hand, from King John. Such were the subsequent confirmations of that charter by succeeding princes. Such was the *petition of right* (author's emphasis) assented to by Charles the First, in the beginning of his reign. Such also, was the declaration of right presented by the lords and commons to the Prince of Orange in 1688, and afterward thrown into the form of an act of parliament, called the bill of rights. It is evident, therefore, that according to their primitive signification, they have no application to constitutions professedly founded upon the power of the people and executed by their immediate representatives and servants. Here, in strictness, the people surrender nothing; and as they retain everything, they have no need of particular reservations. "WE THE PEOPLE of the United States, to secure the blessings of liberty to ourselves and our posterity do *ordain* and *establish* (author's emphasis) this constitution for the United States of America;" This is a better recognition of popular rights, than volumes of those aphorisms, which make the principal figure in several of our state bills of rights, and which would sound much better in a treatise of ethics,

than in a constitution of government.[16]

Hamilton is saying that bills of rights originated in a period when government held unlimited power (via the divine right of kings). They represented a small, first attempt to carve out an area of liberty. The assumption made with a bill of rights is that the government has all power except those "reservations of rights" enumerated in the bill. While such bills were real advancements in the early struggle for liberty, by 1788 Americans had outgrown them. By 1788 liberty was not limited to the particular rights in a given list; liberty had swelled to encompass the entire political universe. It was the powers of government which were limited to a particular enumeration. "Here, in strictness, the people surrender nothing; and as they retain everything, they have no need of particular reservations."[17]

To add a bill of rights to the U.S. Constitution might cause a terrible confusion. It might cause people to think that we were back in that early era when government held all powers except those enumerated in the bill and thus be used to infer a giant, unwarranted expansion of the powers of government. Hamilton continues:

> I go further, and affirm, that bills of rights, in the sense and to the extent they are contended for, are not only unnecessary in the proposed constitution, but would even be dangerous. *They would contain various exceptions to powers not granted, and on this very account would afford a colorable pretext to claim more than were granted. For why declare that things shall not be done which there is no power to do?* Why, for instance, should it be said that the liberty of the press shall not be restrained, when no power is given by which restrictions may be imposed? I will not contend that such a provision would confer a regulating power; but it is evident that it would furnish, to men disposed to usurp, a plausible pretense for claiming that power. They might urge with a semblance of reason that the constitution ought not to be charged with the absurdity of providing against the abuse of an authority, which was not given, and that the provision against restraining the liberty of the press afforded a clear implication, that a right to prescribe proper regulations concerning it, was intended to be vested in the national government. This may serve

as a specimen of the numerous handles which would be given to the doctrine of constructive powers, by the indulgence of an injudicious zeal for bills of rights.[18]

Hamilton's fears came true. Over 80 years after his warning, the very argument he warned against—the doctrine of constructive powers—was made by Justice Strong.

Paradoxically, Marshall adopted his doctrine of implied powers from an argument by Hamilton. Hamilton's plan for a national bank (on the model of William Paterson's Bank of England) was challenged as to constitutionality. In arguing for his bank Hamilton held that *means to a constitutional end* were themselves constitutional. "That every power vested in a government is in its nature *sovereign* and includes, by *force* of the *term* a right to employ all the *means* requisite and fairly applicable to the attainment of the ends of such power. . . ."[19] Thus Hamilton claimed a new set of powers for the Federal Government, which he called implied powers, and which constituted means to a constitutionally valid end. "It is conceded that *implied powers* are to be considered as delegated equally with *express ones.*"[20]

Thomas Jefferson was alarmed at this new doctrine (as in the light of history he might well have been). He felt that Hamilton was opening a Pandora's box of powers. He responded: "I consider the foundation of the Constitution as laid on this ground—that *all powers not delegated to the United States, by the Constitution, nor prohibited by it to the states, are reserved to the states, or to the people.* To take a single step beyond the boundaries thus specially drawn around the powers of Congress, is to take possession of a boundless field of power, no longer susceptible of any definition."[21]

To put a boundry around this concept of powers which were a means to some other end Jefferson invented the doctrine of strict constructionism. He seized upon the last of the powers given to Congress, the power, stated in Art. I, Sect. 8 of the Constitution: "To make all Laws which shall be necessary and proper for carrying into Execution the foregoing Powers. . . ." Jefferson argued that this restricted the government to only *necessary and proper* means and construed the word "necessary" in a strict sense to mean absolutely necessary. ". . . yet the Constitution allows only the means which are 'necessary', not those which are merely 'convenient', for effecting the enumerated powers. If such a latitude of construction be allowed to this phrase as to give any non-enumerated power, it will go to every one; for there is no one which ingenuity may not torture into a *convenience, in some way or other, to some one* of so long a list of enumerated powers. It would swallow up all the delegated powers. It would reduce the whole to one phrase, as before observed. Therefore it was that the Constitution restrained them to the necessary means; that is to say, to those means without which the grant of the power would be nugatory. . . ."[22] Hamilton differed with Jefferson as to the meaning of the word "necessary." He said: "It is certain, that neither the grammatical nor popular sense of the term requires that construction. According to both, *necessary* often means no more than *needful, requisite, incidental, useful,* or *conducive to.* . . ."[23] He thus favored a loose construction of the word "necessary."

But what of Jefferson's fears? Does the Constitution really allow a "boundless field of power, no longer susceptible of any definition?" Almost anything can be regarded as a means to some constitutionally listed end. Three decades ago the U.S. Government gathered up all Japanese-Americans and threw them into concentration camps. This was defended as a means to win the war. The power of Congress to declare war is clearly constitutional, and the imprisonment of the Japanese-Americans was a means to that end. Was it constitutional? Can any American citizen be thrown into a concentration camp because of his racial origin irrespective of proof that he is guilty of a crime? If so, what is the point of having a Constitution?

If *any means* to the enumerated powers are to be regarded as constitutional, then the government can do anything, and there is no point in writing a Constitution to mark out how much it can do. It could put to death all capitalists and seize their wealth to pay the national debt under the power to "pay the debts . . . of the United States." It could jail all members of labor unions under the interstate commerce clause. It could execute all Negroes or Jews or Italians or WASPs or members of any other racial or religious minority, seize all their property, and use it for a road building program under the power "to establish . . . post roads." In short, if this had been the intent of the Founding Fathers, they would not have bothered to write a constitution enumerating the powers of the government; they would simply have said: "The government can do anything it thinks is desirable."

On the other hand some means, not specified in the Constitution, must be allowed if the government is to function. Marshall had argued: "It is not denied that the powers given to the government imply the ordinary means of execution. That for example, of raising revenue, and applying it to national purposes, is admitted to imply the power of conveying money from place to place, as the exigencies of the nation may require, and of employing the usual means of conveyance. . . . Take, for example, the power 'to establish post offices and post roads.' This power is executed by the single act of making the establishment. But from this has been inferred the power and duty of carrying the mail along the post road, from one post office to another."[24] These certainly seem to be reasonable powers, but they are not enumerated in the Constitution.

The solution to this problem is to keep in mind what a constitution is all about. The point at issue when discussing a constitution is the rights of the citizens versus the powers of the government. If an action of government does not interfere with the rights of a citizen, then there is no problem involved. The government can perform that action legitimately. But if an action of government does interfere with the rights of a citizen, then the citizen must have given up that right to the government; he must have given the government the power to interfere with his rights in this area. Since the Constitution is the document by which the people give up some of their liberties to the government, the power must be listed in the Constitution to be legitimate.

This is the answer to the doctrine of implied powers and the resolution of the conflict between strict constructionists and loose constructionists. With regard to actions of government which do not interfere with the rights of the citizen, the government has a free hand. (Just as you and I and any private organization have a free hand to act as we see fit provided we do not interfere with the rights of others.) In these cases the loose constructionists are right; the government can do as it pleases. But when the government interferes with the rights of its citizens, it must first have obtained their grant of power to do so, and such a grant was made by the Constitution. In this case, if the power is not in the Constitution, it has not been granted.

The powers which Marshall uses as examples, to convey money and mail, are clearly not in violation of anyone's rights. Therefore, there was no need for the Constitutional Convention to grant them. Anyone has these powers; therefore the government has , them. But the power to throw a racial minority into concentration camps and the power to force people to accept worthless paper in lieu of a true value do violate people's rights. Therefore, in order for these powers to be valid, they must be enumerated in the Constitution.

And, of course, they are not.

That this is true follows from the nature of constitutional government. But it is interesting to note that Hamilton understood it to be true and never intended the doctrine of implied powers to be used as Marshall and Strong used it. If we go back and look at his full statement: "That every power vested in a government is in its nature sovereign, and includes by *force* of the *term* a right to employ all the *means* requisite and fairly applicable to the attainment of the ends of such power, and which are not precluded by restrictions and exceptions specified in the Constitution, or not immoral, or not contrary to the essential ends of political society. . . ."[25] Hamilton had included two additional requirements before a means could be considered as an implied power, that it be: 1. "not immoral" and 2. "not contrary to the essential ends of political society." The essential end of political society is the protection of rights; acts of government which violate rights are both immoral and contrary to this essential end.

This was only to be expected. It was hardly likely that Hamilton in 1791 would contradict Hamilton in 1788.

The argument between those opposing a bill of rights (on the grounds that it would tend to disparage all rights not listed) and those favoring a bill of rights was resolved in an interesting way. When James Madison offered the Bill of Rights to the first Congress, he was sensitive to the argument that enumerating certain rights would form a pretext for denying those not enumerated, and, as he said, "I conceive, that it may be guarded against. . . ." Madison's solution was to include the following words in the Bill of Rights: "The exceptions here or elsewhere in the Constitution, made in favor of particular rights, shall not be so construed as to diminish the just importance of other rights retained by the people, or as to enlarge the powers delegated by the Constitution; but either as actual limitations of such powers, or as inserted merely for greater caution."[26] This would meet Hamilton's fears by specifically eliminating any implication of a doctrine of constructive powers. It was simplified by committee to: "The enumeration in the Constitution of certain rights shall not be construed to deny or disparage others retained by the people. . . . The powers not delegated to the United States by the Constitution, nor prohibited by it to the States are reserved to the States respectively or to the people." These passed into law as the ninth and tenth amendments to the Constitution.

So the Founding Fathers not only disagreed with Justice Strong's theory of "powers . . . which grew out of the aggregate," they wrote their opinion into the Constitution where it remains the supreme law of the land to this day. And any judgement rendered which does not take cognizance of this can make no claim to be either legal or constitutional. It has no legitimate authority.

It is interesting to note the following debate. The Constitutional Convention never discussed the issue of paper money directly. The pro-paper money faction was such a small minority that it did not dare to bring up the issue for a vote. However, a back door attempt to smuggle in paper money was made via the power to issue bills of credit. Technically bills of credit are a short term means of borrowing (like Treasury bills today). But in practice at the time they were often made legal tender. The paper money forces hoped to persuade the Convention to adopt the bills of credit power by pretending that nothing more was involved than the power to borrow for short periods of time. Then, when the power was safely enacted, they would turn around and say: "Of course, bills of credit are always made legal tender; that was what was intended. Everyone realized that when they voted for the power." The failure of this subterfuge sheds some light on the intention of the Founding Fathers. Here is the actual debate at the Constitutional Convention in 1787:

> Mr. Gouverneur Morris moved to strike out, "and emit bills on the credit of the United States." If the United States had credit, such bills would be unnecessary; if they had not, unjust and useless.
>
> Mr. Butler seconds the motion.
>
> Mr. Madison. Will it not be sufficient to prohibit the making them a *tender* (author's emphasis)? This will remove the temptation to emit them with unjust views. And promissory notes, in that shape, may in some emergencies be best.

At this point in the debate the pretext of bills of credit was dropped, and the Convention began to debate the real issue—paper money.

> Mr. Gourverneur Morris. Striking out the words will leave room still for notes of a *responsible* (author's emphasis) minister, which will do all the good without the mischief. The moneyed interest will oppose the plan of government, *if paper emissions be not prohibited.*
>
> Mr. Gorham was for striking out without inserting any prohibition. If the words stand, they may suggest and lead to the measure.
>
> Mr. Mason had doubts on the subject. *Congress, he thought, would not have the power, unless it were expressed.* Though he had a mortal hatred to paper-money, yet as he could not foresee all emergencies, he was unwilling to tie the hands of the Legislature. He observed that the late war could not have been carried on, had such a prohibition existed.
>
> Mr. Gorham. The power, as far as it will be necessary, or safe, is involved in that of borrowing.
>
> Mr. Mercer was a friend to paper-money, though in the present state and temper of America, he should neither propose nor approve of such a measure. *He was consequently opposed to a prohibition of it altogether.* It will stamp suspicion on the Government, to deny it a discretion on this point. It was impolitic, also, to excite the opposition of all those who were friends to paper-money. The people of property would be sure to be on the side of the plan, and it was impolitic to purchase their

further attachment with the loss of the opposite class of citizens.

Mr. Ellsworth thought this a favorable moment, *to shut and bar the door against paper-money*. The mischiefs of the various experiments which had been made were now fresh in the public mind, and had excited the disgust of all the respectable part of America. *By withholding the power from the new Government,* more friends of influence would be gained to it than by almost any thing else. Paper-money can in no case be necessary. Give the Government credit, and other resources will offer. The power may do harm, never good.

Mr. Randolph, notwithstanding his antipathy to paper-money, could not agree to strike out the words, as he could not foresee all the occasions that might arise.

Mr. Wilson. It will have a most salutary influence on the credit of the United States, *to remove the possibility of paper-money*. This expedient can never succeed whilst its mischiefs are remembered. And as long as it can be resorted to, it will be a bar to other resources.

Mr. Butler remarked, that paper was a legal tender in no country in Europe. He was urgent for *disarming the government of such a power.*

Mr. Mason was still averse to tying the hands of the Legislature *altogether* (author's emphasis). If there was no example in Europe, as just remarked, it might be observed on the other side, that there was none in which the Government was restrained on this head.

Mr. Read thought the words, if not struck out, would be as alarming as the mark of the Beast in Revelation.

Mr. Langdon had rather reject the whole plan, than retain the three words, "and emit bills."

On the motion for striking out,—New Hampshire, Massachusetts, Connecticut, Pennsylvania, Delaware, Virginia*, North Carolina, South Carolina, Georgia, aye - 9; New Jersey, Maryland, no - 2.

*This vote in the affirmative by Virginia was occasioned by the acquiescence of Mr. Madison, who became satisfied that striking out the words would not disable the Government from the use of public notes, as far as they could be safe and proper; and would only cut off the pretext for a *paper-currency* (author's emphasis) and particularly for making the bills a *tender* (author's emphasis) either for public or private debts.[27]

In other words, the authors of the Constitution refused to give the Federal Government power to issue bills of credit because they were afraid these bills would be used as a pretext for paper money. They did this, not by inserting a prohibition against bills of credit but by omitting to grant the government the power to issue them. Even those of the delegates who favored paper money understood that, if the power were not granted, it would not exist.

The good citizen, whose concern is to do right and obey the law, must be very concerned with this question of legitimate authority. The government of the United States has legitimate authority because it is based on a constitution in which powers are given to it by the voluntary consent of the people. But this fact means that it has no legitimate authority with regard to powers that it usurps.

When the government usurps powers, then it is acting illegitimately, like a murderer or thief. The good citizen owes no obedience to usurpations. Usurpations are not law. No act of Congress made outside of the powers given to it by the Constitution is valid.

Supporters of authority today argue that the Supreme Court "interprets" the Constitution. They claim that the Supreme Court was set up as the highest authority to decide what the Constitution means.

Such an institution would have been totally alien to the concepts of the Founding Fathers. They intended the judiciary as the weakest of the three branches of government. They meant the Constitution to be the supreme law, binding on everyone and regarded it as the moral obligation of every good citizen to obey the Constitution.

In their eyes this meant that the good citizen had an obligation to study the Constitution, come to *his own understanding* of what it meant, and act on that understanding. This is what George Washington did when faced with Hamilton's plan for a central bank. He did not say, "I'll leave the constitutionality up to the Supreme Court." Instead he solicited opinions from opposing sides and made up his mind on the merits.

The proper function of the Supreme Court (and the lower courts) is to resolve disputes in accordance with the law, the Constitution being supreme law. In this function it has a moral responsibility to interpret words and phrases in the Constitution to the best of its ability and to rule in accordance. But this function is not unique. The President has a moral responsibility to act in accordance with the law and (as in the case of Washington) must try to interpret words and phrases in the Constitution to the best of *his* ability. Every Congressman in voting has an obligation not to enact unconstitutional laws; thus he also must interpret words and phrases in the Constitution. The point here is that no one person's interpretation of the Constitution was made absolute.

Some people of the time opposed the Constitution on precisely the grounds that the Supreme Court was being made into an absolute authority. Hamilton paraphrased their arguments as follows: " 'The authority of the proposed Supreme Court of the United States, which is to be a separate and independent body, will be superior to that of the legislature. The power of construing the laws according to the *spirit* of the Constitution will enable that court to mould them into whatever shape it may think proper; especially as its decisions will not be in any manner subject to the revision or correction of the legislative body. This is as unprecedented as it is dangerous.' "[28] Hamilton rebuts this point of view, saying: "This, upon examination, will be found to be made up altogether of false reasoning upon misconceived fact."[29] And he goes on to discuss the power of impeachment as a remedy for Supreme Court justices who abuse the Constitution.

There are people today who have such a love of authority and fear of using their own judgement that they must search for authority figures where none exist. These people wish to make the Supreme Court into the Pope of the American Constitution. In their view the Supreme Court is the highest authority on the Constitution just as the Pope is the highest authority on the Bible.

The Founding Fathers did not count on a supreme authority to maintain liberty. They knew that liberty cannot survive under a supreme authority. They placed their hopes on a balance of power. If *all* elements of society had the responsibility to interpret and uphold the Constitution, then the resulting system, while it might result in specific injustices, could never get too badly out of gear. Their intention was that each person should make his own judgement on the Constitution and then act on that judgement in terms of whatever actions were appropriate.

I am not here arguing that people should disobey whatever decision of the Supreme Court they do not like. There is a certain value to order and stability, and sometimes it is wiser to submit to an isolated injustice than to create a turmoil to correct it. But, as the Declaration of Independence points out: ". . . mankind are more disposed to suffer, while evils are sufferable, than to right themselves by abolishing the forms to which they are accustomed." When there occurs such a travesty of justice as the legal tender decision of 1871 where the Court was packed for partisan purposes, where it is clear that the Court never seriously intended to be bound by the Constitution, where the judges ignored the explicit words of the Constitutional Convention on the subject, then it is time to return to first principles and say: The *Constitution* is the supreme law; the decision of 1871 was a miscarriage of justice, and whatever practical effect it had on the people of the time, it is not *law,* and it is not binding on us today. We are bound by law under the Constitution, not by decisions made in opposition to the Constitution. The legal tender acts are usurpations; they are not law; and they have no legitimate authority.

The Civil War attempt at fiat money did not succeed. It was left for a later day and age to accomplish that. The railroads did get to pay off much of their debt in depreciated paper, but when the war hysteria abated, the pro-gold forces regained control. The money supply was gradually brought into line with the quantity of gold, and redemption of the greenback into gold was established in 1879. Meanwhile people wrote into their private contracts explicit provisions that, whatever the legal tender, payment was to be made in gold coin. The gold standard was resumed.

It is interesting to note that this period, which was largely one of declining prices (partly caused by the contraction in the money supply necessary to resume the gold standard and partly caused by the switch from a bimetallic standard—where both gold and silver were used as money—to a pure gold standard) was the greatest period of economic expansion of any country in the history of civilization. From the end of the Civil War to the turn of the century the country underwent an economic revolution the like of which had never been seen before and has not been seen since. A host of technological improvements, *whose benefits were speedily made available to the average man,* flowed from the minds of the creative members of society. A continent was conquered, tamed and settled. *And the real wages (in terms of constant dollars) of the average worker more than doubled.* (The contrast with our recent past can hardly be more vivid.)

It was not until another period of hysteria in the country—that of the great depression and the run on the banks—that the gold standard was finally abrogated permanently. Again it was by a Supreme Court decision of five to four made under extreme conditions. In this case (*Nortz v. United States,* decided in the term of October 1934) the right to own gold was denied and even contracts made with an explicit gold coin clause were abrogated. When Senator Carter Glass, who had been instrumental in writing the Democratic platform of 1932, first heard of this bill, he said: "It's dishonor, Sir. This great Government, strong in gold, is breaking its promises to pay gold to widows and orphans to whom it has sold Government bonds with a pledge to pay gold coin of the present standard of value. It is breaking its promise to redeem its paper money in gold coin of the present standard of value. It's dishonor, Sir."[30]

The argument was, of course, the doctrine of implied powers (á la Marshall). There is no hint of any power in the Constitution to prohibit the ownership of gold or to enact the blanket abrogation of contracts. Alexander Hamilton would not have agreed with this decision. He had written: "When a government enters into a contract with an individual, it deposes, as to the matter of the contract, its constitutional authority, and exchanges the character of the legislator for that of a moral agent, with the same rights and obligations as an individual. Its promises may be justly considered as excepted out of its power to legislate, unless in aid of them. It is in theory impossible to reconcile the idea of a promise which obliges, with a power to make a law which can vary the effect of it."[31] In this case the paper money forces were a little more explicit.

as to their beliefs. The Government argued the medieval doctrine of unlimited sovereignty:

> If the court please, other nations, impelled by the requirements of necessity and acting for the public welfare, have devalued their currencies, abandoned the gold standard, and abrogated gold contracts by specific laws enacted for that purpose. Without challenge and without question they have done precisely what the Congress of the United States has done. Belgium, France, Germany, Rumania, Mexico, Norway, and Sweden have enacted such laws. It is an essential attribute of sovereignty.
>
> I ask this court to lay down in unequivocal language the proposition that, in matters of currency, the courses of action open to other governments are not denied to this country, and that, in employing these sovereign powers, we act upon an equality with all the other nations of the earth.[32]

Sovereign means: "Above or superior to all others; chief; greatest; supreme."[33] In America the people are sovereign. The Government is the servant, not the master, of the people. It is not for nothing that the preamble to the Constitution states: "We the people of the United States . . . do ordain and establish this Constitution." Hamilton cited this statement in his argument against a bill of rights because he wanted to emphasize that it was the *people,* who are originally sovereign, who delegated a *portion* of their liberties to the government. But in 1935 this principle was thrown out in order to imitate, as the government attorney put it, "Germany, Rumania, Mexico."

The government attorney would not admit it, but he had turned back the clock and was invoking the doctrine of the divine right of kings, which goes: (1) God gives special powers to the king; (2) Who thereby has authority (sovereignty) over the people. This directly contradicts the Founding Fathers who believed that liberty inheres in people and that the people delegate authority to the government. The government attorney did not dare to invoke the first premise of the divine right of kings argument, but he is quite explicit about the second. He wants us to admit that the government has sovereign powers not delegated to it by the people, not because it got them from God, but just because, well . . . , everybody else has them, so why the heck not.

The attorney for the government could not have known it, but his enumeration of countries for the U.S. to imitate was most revealing in its inclusion of Germany, then under its new leader, Adolf Hitler. That Hitler immediately debauched the currency and instituted strict price and wage controls (see Chapter VIII) was not an accident. It was the natural concomitant of a social theory which exalted the destroyer of values (the warrior) and denigrated the producer. That Nazi Germany should have been held up as an example for the United States to follow in this regard is an eloquent comment on the nature of paper money.

FOOTNOTES

[1] Daniel Webster as quoted by Chief Justice Salmon P. Chase, "Supreme Court Reports," *Legal Tender Cases*, 12 Wall 586, Opinion of the Minority, Chase's emphasis.

[2] As quoted by Sidney Ratner, "Was the Supreme Court Packed by President Grant?" *Political Science Quarterly*, Sept. 1935, pp. 343-58.

[3] Andrew C. McLaughlin, Wilson on Blackstone, *The Foundations of American Constitutionalism* (New York, 1932), pp. 83-84.

[4] "Constitution of Mass., 1780," chiefly the work of John Adams, from *Documents of American History*, 8th Edition, ed. Henry Steele Commager (New York, 1968), p. 107.

[5] Author unknown, *Four Letters on Interesting Subjects*, letter IV (Philadelphia, 1776), p. 19, Author's emphasis.

[6] Daniel Webster, as quoted by Clarkson Nott Potter, Supreme Court Reports, *Legal Tender Cases (Knox v. Lee & Parker v. Davis)*, 12 Wall 495.

[7] Daniel Webster, as quoted by Chief Justice Salmon P. Chase, *Op. Cit.*

[8] James Madison, *The Federalist Papers* (New York, 1961), No. 10, p. 84.

[9] James Madison, in a letter to Edmund Randolph, Philadelphia, May 14, 1782, from *Madison Papers* (Washington, 1840), I, p. 129, on the prospect of Virginia issuing paper money.

[10] Thomas Jefferson, "Notes on the Establishment of a Money Unit, and of a Coinage for the United States," *Memoir, Correspondence and Misc.*, (Boston, 1830), ed. T. Randolph, Vol. I, 2nd Ed., pp. 138-9.

[11] *The Records of the Federal Convention of 1787*, ed. Max Farrand (New Haven, 1937), I, p. 154.

[12] *Ibid.*, Yates on Madison.

FOOTNOTES (Cont.)

[13] *Ibid.,* Vol. III, p. 214. Martin's emphasis.

[14] Justice Strong, Supreme Court Reports, *Legal Tender Cases,* 12 Wall 534-35, Opinion of the Court.

[15] John Marshall, Supreme Court Reports, *McCullough v. The State of Maryland,* Opinion of the Court, 4 Wheaton 421.

[16] Alexander Hamilton, *The Federalist Papers* (New York, 1961), No. 84, pp. 512-13. [My emphasis except where noted.]

[17] *Ibid.*

[18] *Ibid.,* pp. 513-14.

[19] Alexander Hamilton, "Opinion on the Constitutionality of the Bank," Feb. 23, 1791, *Documents of American History, Op. Cit.,* pp. 156-57. Author's emphasis.

[20] *Ibid.*

[21] Thomas Jefferson, "Opinion on the Constitutionality of the Bank," Feb. 15, 1791, *Documents of American History, Ibid.,* pp. 159-60. Author's emphasis.

[22] *Ibid.*

[23] Hamilton, "Opinion. . . ," *Op. Cit.,* p. 157. Author's emphasis.

[24] John Marshall, *Op. Cit.*

[25] Hamilton, "Opinion. . . ," *Op. Cit.,* p. 156. Author's emphasis.

[26] James Madison, speech in the House of Representatives on June 8, 1789, *Debates and Proceedings in the Congress of the United States,* (Washington, Gales & Seaton, 1834), Vol. I, p. 439.

[27] *The Madison Papers,* III (Washington, 1840), record of Aug. 16, 1787, pp. 1343-46 [My emphasis except where noted.]

[28] Alexander Hamilton, *The Federalist Papers* (New York, 1961), #81, p. 482.

[29] *Ibid.*

[30] Sen. Carter Glass, as quoted in *Economics and the Public Welfare,* Benjamin M. Anderson (New York, 1949), p. 317.

[31] Alexander Hamilton, as quoted in Supreme Court Reports, Opinion of the minority, *Gold Clause Cases (Norman v. Baltimore & Ohio R. Co., United States v. Bankers Trust Co., Nortz v. United States,* and *Perry v. United States),* 294 U.S. 379-80.

[32] Supreme Court Reports, Argument for the Government, *Norman v. B&O. R. Co.,* 294 U.S. 272.

[33] *Webster's New World Dictionary, College Edition* (New York, World, 1960), p. 1395.

CHAPTER VII

"How You Can Profit From The Coming..."

There is a school of thought—principally the followers of Ludwig Von Mises—which is well aware of the dangers of paper money. Although they are reluctant to attack the bankers and big business, their analysis of economic causes and effects is accurate.

The best exposition of this point of view is Harry Browne's book, *How You Can Profit from the Coming Devaluation,* which I recommend highly for a clear explanation of the monetary situation. However, Mr. Browne claims that you, as an individual, may protect yourself from paper money by an investment program. With this I must disagree. There is no way to fight the bankers as an individual. The alternatives faced by the country are continuing depreciation of the currency at a greater and greater rate or a currency stabilization or contraction.

It is true that there is an investment program which will enable you to profit from the depreciation of the currency. It consists of, in effect, joining the bankers. It encourages you to go into debt; it advises you to hold common stocks (except for gold stocks), with a seasoning of the more risky groups; it recommends real estate and does not look askance on such investments as rare coins and art.

Similarly, there is an investment program for a period of stabilization in the value of the currency. It tells you to avoid common stocks except for very conservative investments and gold stocks. It recommends putting your money into bonds and savings accounts, and, for those inclined to greater risk, allows a little short selling.

The point is that these two investment programs are mutually exclusive. What will benefit from depreciation will be harmed by stabilization and vice versa. There is no investment program which will protect one from all possibilities.

I have observed that people tend to make their investments in accord with their political convictions. Because the investment program of the banking establishment has proven so successful over the past 40 years, it has lured many people into buying into this kind of a program and thus acquiring a vested interest in the depreciation of the currency. These people, like those whose jobs are dependent on currency depreciation, have a vested interest in a course of action which will lead to the destruction of the nation.

The point I wish to make here is that no individual can stand aside and save himself. There is no way to ensure one's economic survival while everyone else's wealth is expropriated by the aristocracy. If the President will expand the money supply, cut the final tie between our currency and gold, and enact price and wage controls for these people, then he will pass other laws which they find necessary, and since it is impossible for them to profit without your losing, you will be robbed in one way or another.

One cannot even gain by joining the bankers, not in the long run. In the first place, if one does, then a victory by the sound money forces will leave one poorer. In the second place, as the depreciation progresses, it wipes out the wealth of the productive members of the society, and the members of the establishment are forced to devour one another.

An example of this occurred in early 1969. At that time the "New Breed" on Wall Street—those adopting their business practices to extreme issues of paper money—were taking over numerous established companies. The management of these companies—who had been running their businesses on the traditional basis of mild issues of paper money—were threatened. When James Ling took over Jones and Laughlin, an old line steel company, it sent a chill through the powers-that-be in the business community. Who would be next? What was needed was a good dose of sound money. It would hurt the establishment. But it would totally destroy the "New Breed." I cannot help but think that the influence of this group of people—some of the wealthiest and most powerful men in the country—was responsible for the determination of the Nixon administration to fight "inflation" in 1969. Surely, after the "New Breed" had been destroyed, the Nixon administration reversed its position quickly enough. Thus the best explanation for the 1970 recession and slowing of the rate of "inflation" which it produced is that it represented a battle between the present establishment and the "New Breed" for economic and political power in this country. In this battle the "New Breed" was defeated, as the establishment thought it better to take slightly lower profits for a few years in order that their challengers might be put down. On such considerations does the economic condition of the country depend.

No individual, as an individual, can protect himself from the ravages of the bankers. So long as the government will do their bidding, all our wealth can be expropriated at any time. There is no place to hide where you can sit out the storm while everyone else is destroyed. There is only one way to fight against the bankers. We must join together through the political process and wrest from them their power to exploit us. We must elect men to public office who oppose paper money. We are, by far, the majority in this country. All who labor and all who save are on our side. When we have recognized this truth, no one can stop us.

Those who join the fight may take heart from another incident in American history. The Revolutionary War was fought with paper money which depreciated greatly and which had the usual effect in enriching members of the banking establishment of the time. "The expanding currency and consequent depreciation in the value of money had immediately resulted in a corresponding rise of prices, which for a while the States attempted to control. But in 1778 Congress threw up its hands in despair and voted that 'all limitations of prices of gold and silver be taken off,' although the States for some time longer continued to endeavor to regulate prices by legislation. The fluctuating value of the currency increased the opportunities for speculation which war conditions invariably offer, and 'immense fortunes were suddenly accumulated.' A new financial group rose into prominence composed largely of those who were not accustomed to the use of money and who were consequently inclined to spend it recklessly and extravagantly."[1] exactly as happened in 1967-68.

But after the War, when the paper money ceased, there was a contraction which bore most heavily on the "new financial group." "Closely associated with the coinage problem was the paper-money situation in the states. In some, new taxes permitted the partial retirement of bills and improved the credit of what remained; but the depression, as we have seen, brought fresh demands for inflation which reached their climax in 1785 and 1786."[2] exactly as happened in 1970-71.

But the good men of that time did not give up in despair as Harry Browne advises. They did not retire from the public arena to devise plans to save their individual fortunes while the country went to pieces. They banded together through the political process and devised a plan which would put an end to paper money. This plan consisted of forming a strong central government which would prohibit the State governments from issuing paper money. Its document of implementation was the Constitution. The character of the two contending parties of the time (Federalist and anti-Federalist) has been described by Justice John Marshall:

> At length two great parties were formed in every state which were distinctly marked and which pursued distinct objects with systematic arrangement. The one struggled with unabated zeal for the exact observance of public and private engagements. By those belonging to it, the faith of a nation or of a private man was deemed a sacred pledge, the violation of which was equally forbidden by the principles of moral justice and of sound policy. The distresses of individuals were, they thought to be alleviated only by industry and frugality, not by a relaxation of the laws or by a sacrifice of the rights of others. They were consequently the uniform friends of a regular administration of justice, and of a vigorous course of taxation which would enable the state to comply with its engagements. By a natural association of ideas, they

were also, with very few exceptions, in favor of enlarging the powers of the federal government.

The other party marked out for themselves a more indulgent course. Viewing with extreme tenderness the case of the debtor, their efforts were unceasingly directed to his relief. To exact a faithful compliance with contracts was, in their opinion, a harsh measure which the people would not bear. They were uniformly in favor of relaxing the administration of justice, of affording facilities for the payment of debts, or of suspending their collection, and of remitting taxes. The same course of opinion led them to resist every attempt to transfer from their own hands into those of congress powers which by others were deemed essential to the preservation of the union. In many of these states the party last mentioned constituted a decided majority of the people, and in all of them it was very powerful. The emission of paper money, the delay of legal proceedings, and the suspension of the collection of taxes were the fruits of their rule wherever they were completely predominant.[3]

To defeat the paper money forces the Federalists called a convention in the summer of 1787 to propose a more extensive grant of powers to the federal government.

In contrast to the cheap-money victories in several commonwealths was the resistance by conservatives, notably in New England outside Rhode Island; in New York, where issues were so restricted as to prevent serious depreciation; and in the Chesapeake states, where inflationist sentiment, though formidable, was ultimately defeated. The popular agitation, however, proved sufficiently disturbing to indicate the need of federal control. So the Federal Convention, composed largely of merchants, lawyers and substantial landowners, readily agreed to place coinage and currency legislation under the exclusive jurisdiction of Congress. While this made the Constitution attractive to the mercantile and financial interests, it antagonized the agrarian and other debtor elements, which came dangerously near defeating ratification.[4]

Dr. David Ramsay, in a pamphlet advocating the ratification of the Constitution, makes it clear just who he expects to be on the other side: "Be on your guard against the misrepresentations of men who are involved in debt; such may wish to see the

Constitution rejected because of the following clause, 'no state shall . . . emit bills of credit, make anything but gold and silver coin a tender in payment of debts, pass any . . . ex post facto law, or law impairing the obligation of contracts.' This will doubtless bear hard on debtors who wish to defraud their creditors, but it will be a real service to the honest part of the community."[5] And Charles Beard made this the major point of his economic interpretation of the Constitution:

> In addition to being frequently in debt for their lands, the small farmers were dependent on the towns for most of the capital to develop their resources. They were, in other words, a large debtor class, to which must be added, of course, the urban dwellers who were in a like unfortunate condition.
>
> That this debtor class had developed a strong consciousness of identical interests in the several states is clearly evident in local politics and legislation. Shays' Rebellion in Massachusetts, the disturbances in Rhode Island, New Hampshire, and other northern states, the activities of the paper money advocates in state legislatures, the innumerable schemes for the relief of debtors, such as the abolition of imprisonment, paper money, laws delaying the collection of debts, propositions requiring debtors to accept land in lieu of specie at a valuation fixed by a board of arbitration—these and many other schemes testify eloquently to the fact that the debtors were conscious of their status and actively engaged in establishing their interest in the form of legal provisions. Their philosophy was reflected in the writings of Luther-Martin, delegate to the Convention from Maryland, who disapproved of the Constitution, partly on the ground that it would put a stop to agrarian legislation. . . .
>
> Money capital was suffering in two ways under the Articles of Confederation. It was handicapped in seeking profitable outlets by the absence of protection for manufactures, the lack of security in investments in western lands, and discriminations against American shipping by foreign countries. It was also being positively attacked by the makers of paper money, stay laws, pine barren acts, and other devices for depreciating the currency or delaying the collection of debts. In addition there was a widespread derangement of the monetary system and the coinage due

to the absence of uniformity and stability in the standards.

Creditors, naturally enough, resisted all of these schemes in the state legislatures and failing to find relief there at length turned to the idea of a national government so constructed as to prevent laws impairing the obligations of contract, emitting paper money, and otherwise benefiting debtors. It is idle to inquire whether the rapacity of the creditors or the total depravity of the debtors (a matter much discussed at the time) was responsible for this deep and bitter antagonism. It is sufficient for our purposes to discover its existence and to find its institutional reflex in the Constitution.[6]

The above historical context makes it clear that Marshall never intended his doctrine of implied powers to be used to defend paper money. Being a Federalist, he would have had an abhorrence of paper money. According to Beard the main reason for writing the Constitution was to ban such debtor legislation as paper money. Furthermore, the whole thrust of the Federalists' program was to increase the power of the Federal Government at the expense of the States, not at the expense of the individual. In fact what the Federalists were trying to do was to protect the individual from abuse by the state governments. Daniel Shays had demanded an equal division of property, abolition of debts and paper money; in all of these regards he looked to the state government to legislate them. It was to protect people's rights against such threats that section ten of Article I was inserted into the Constitution.

With this historical context, we can see how the aristocracy's arguments have evolved to the present day. 200 years ago the paper money party claimed that they represented the interests of the poor farmer. This claim had two advantages. It won for them the sympathy which one has for the poor, and it had the very practical advantage that the overwhelming majority of people in the country were farmers. Beard swallowed this claim and reported it as historical fact, but it was not true. Anyone familiar with business practice knows that the poor never become big debtors for the simple reason that no one will lend them any significant amounts of money. In any society it is the rich who are the big debtors because it is they who have the lines of credit. Furthermore, if the class lines were as simply drawn as is suggested by

Beard, agrarian versus commercial class, the agrarians would have won overwhelmingly because they were by far the majority. The paper money party was led by the debtor element, people who had bought land on heavy credit playing for a rise and represented themselves as speaking for the farmers. This analysis is confirmed by the fact that the one state where the paper money faction met its greatest success, Rhode Island, was the state with the largest commercial class and the fewest farmers. Thomas Jefferson, writing in 1786, could say, ". . .there is not a single man in Rhode Island who is not a merchant of some sort."[7] While this is doubtless an exaggeration, it makes the point. Rhode Island refused for several years to join the Union because the Constitution prohibited paper money. Jefferson himself, the agrarian *par excellence,* was a devoted hard money man and later led the agrarian class in a fight against the first Bank of the United States. If in the 1780s the interests of the agrarians were served by paper money, it is strange that in the 1790s their interests were served by hard money.

When farmers ceased to be a majority of the population, the political base of the debtors' argument was shattered, and they cast about for another social class to carry their banner. They chose the common laborer. Their argument had two points, which I call the Marxian point and the Keynesian point. The first (Marxian) point was to be pro-labor by advocating raising a worker's wages above the value of his labor. This point is behind the minimum wage legislation and the legislation giving labor unions the power to restrict entry into their field. The effect of this legislation was to create unemployment.

The problem then became to reduce unemployment. The second (Keynesian) point was to be pro-labor and reduce unemployment by lowering wages. Just as raising wages above the value of the worker's labor caused unemployment, so lowering the wages again would reduce it. However, in the political atmosphere of the 1930s it was not considered pro-labor to lower wages outright. Keynes' scheme was to lower the real value of wages by depreciating the currency. He well understood the point that in a currency depreciation prices rise faster than wages, thus lowering the real value of the workers' pay. As he stated: "Every trade union will put up some resistance to a cut in money wages, however small. But since no trade union would dream of striking on every occasion of a rise in the cost of living, they do not raise the obstacle to any increase in aggregate employment which is attributed to them by the classical school."[8] The net result of all these "pro-labor" measures was that wages were reduced again, and the associated vested interests were left with a perfect rationalization for the depreciation of the currency. If someone spoke out against issuing paper money, then he could be condemned as anti-labor because he was "for" unemployment. If he advocated eliminating unemployment by ending the measures which caused it, the minimum wage and the power of unions to restrict entry, he was condemned as anti-labor because he was in favor of lowering wages.

The net effect of the Marxian and Keynesian points was not to leave the worker exactly where he otherwise would have been. The working of the two measures is uneven. Some workers are left with (the obligation to demand) wages above the value of their labor and hence are unemployed. And other workers are left with wages below the value of their labor.

Incredibly, this dual rationalization is extremely common today. The majority of people accept that it is pro-labor to raise wages (causing unemployment) and pro-labor to lower wages by depreciating the currency (to reduce unemployment). The final result of all these pro-labor measures is that bankers, big businessmen and promoters get rich at the expense of the working class.

In the 19th century there were bitter political battles over hard money versus soft money, but the soft money forces of the time have the character of a vested interest. It is not until the 20th century that they begin to take on the characteristics of an aristocracy. This occurred with their adoption of a liberal guise.

Paper money is inherently anti-liberal. It robs from the poor to give to the rich; it is conducive to war; it leads to the centralization of economic power in the hands of a few big corporations; it leads to restrictions on individual freedom. But starting with Wilson the paper money forces in America have gone to great lengths to portray themselves as of the left. It is the "pro-labor" measures of Marx and Keynes which have been the key element in this masquerade.

In all *public and highly visible areas* the Wilson and FDR administrations and their successors adopted leftist measures. But in terms of real effect, their administrations were highly reactionary. (Gabriel Kolko's excellent book *The Triumph of Conservatism* unmasks the real pro-business aspect of the Wilson administration.) Take, for example, the social welfare programs of the New Deal.

The social welfare programs gave the New Deal an extreme left wing image. Such slogans as "Rob from the rich to give to the poor" convinced people that FDR was willing to go to extreme lengths, even in violation of simple justice, to favor the laboring class. The highly public decisions of the National Labor Relations Board were extremely biased in favor of labor and served, quite properly, to outrage the business community. FDR was delighted when his enemies called him "a traitor to his class."

But FDR was not a traitor to his class. Let us do a little economic calculation. It was the social programs which won liberal support for the Roosevelt budget deficits. Important elements of the liberal community started supporting budget deficits in the 1930s on the (correct) political observation that it was easier to put across some additional social programs when spending could exceed income.

These liberals should go back and do their economic homework. The original American liberals, men such as Thomas Jefferson and Andrew Jackson, took the exact opposite position. Jefferson and Jackson were hard money men and against paper money whether it was legal tender or a central bank promoting the smaller banks in their lending of money which does not exist. Jefferson and Jackson understood that the transfer of wealth from poor to rich which occurs from the factors described in Chapter III far dwarfs the transfer from rich to poor from any social programs. They took the side of the common man by supporting hard money and opposing the paper money issued by the Bank of the United States. The next time that modern liberals toast these men at an annual dinner they should stop and do a little calculation.

Assume a budget deficit of $20 billion which leads to a currency depreciation of 6%. This is in reasonable conformity with recent experience. Of this $20 billion, perhaps $10 billion may go to social programs, the rest going to things like a space shuttle or aid to Lockheed, etc. Of the $10 billion perhaps $2 to $3 billion may work its way down through the bureaucracy and actually get to the poor.

Total debt in the U.S. is now about $2 trillion. (That is, $2 thousand billion.) If the currency depreciated by 6% and the rate of interest did not rise to discount the depreciation, this would result in a transfer of wealth from creditor to debtor amounting to $120 billion.

More realistically let us assume that the rate of interest has risen 3% above what it otherwise would have been to discount the depreciation. That is, of the 6% currency depreciation, 3% is compensated for by an increase in interest rates and 3% represents a transfer of wealth from creditor to debtor. (The fact that interest rates do not rise fully to compensate for the currency depreciation is due to the intervention of the Federal Reserve.) If we take 3% times $2 trillion, we get $60 billion transferred from creditors to debtors by the depreciation of the currency.

The major debtors in the U.S. today (as in all countries in all times) are the big corporations. It is they who have the lines of credit from the banks. The major creditors are the thrifty middle class who save small amounts for a rainy day; this especially applies to the elderly who are now living off their savings, many of whom have been reduced to poverty by the recent currency depreciation.

Thus to secure a $2 to $3 billion transfer of wealth from the rich to the poor, modern liberals help create a $60 billion transfer of wealth, most of which is from the poor and middle classes to the rich. This $60 billion figure, large as it is, does not even begin to measure the transfer of wealth from poor to rich due to a depreciation of the currency because it does not include the loss in real wages due to the fact that wages do not rise as rapidly as prices nor does it include the money coaxed from the gullible by Wall Street promoters.

It is instructive to compare the past 35 years in American economic history, which have been a period of continually rising prices, with the period from 1865 to 1900, a period of continually falling prices. In the past 35 years, we are taught, the country has been extremely pro-labor. Unions have grown in size and power. The dominant political party identifies itself as the party of the working man. Politicians swear their allegiance to labor. During this period the gain in real wages has been about 50%. In the period from 1865 to 1900, we are taught, the country was extremely anti-labor. Business was ruled by the Robber Barons. There were only tiny unions with little power, and even these were often surpressed by the police or National Guard. Yet during this period the gain in real wages was over 100%.

The reason is, of course, that a currency depreciation lowers wages and a currency appreciation raises wages. Keynes understood this and devised an economic theory which on the surface was pro-labor but which opened the door for paper money. Taken as an economic theory with a long record of failure, Keynesianism is very unimpressive. One is led to wonder what an intelligent man like Keynes was doing espousing such foolish theory. But taken as dogma for a modern priesthood—as a set of myths to enable modern economists to fool the public into accepting their own exploitation—Keynesian economics is a work of art.

Like any good confidence man Keynes had a sharp ear for the prejudices and biases of the people of his time. By the early 20th century, liberalism was dominant. Science, progress and humanism were the values which were esteemed. By dressing his economic theories up in a scientific and liberal guise Keynes was able to convince people of their validity.

Keynesian economics is in fact a return to 17th century mercantilism. It comes to conclusions long since refuted by the 18th and 19th century economic greats—Adam Smith, Jean Baptiste Say, Frédéric Bastiat and others. It is an economic theory which belongs in the age of dukes and kings. Yet Keynes took these ideas, old in the year 1800, and presented them as the "New Economics." He took a set of beliefs which rationalize an aristocracy and presented it as the latest in liberal thought. He defended a system which robs from the poor and gives to the rich and yet postured as a friend of the poor. He advocated the theory that something can be created from nothing, yet he posed as a believer in science and an opponent of mysticism.

Although Keynes' conclusions are very close to the economic

conclusions of fascism, he always maintained his image as a liberal. This was necessary as Keynes needed liberal support to put his ideas across. Yet there was one occasion when he was willing to lift the mask a little. In his introduction to the *German* (but not the English) edition of his book "General Theory of Employment, Interest and Money," Keynes wrote: "The theory of aggregate production, which is the point of the following book, nevertheless can be much easier adapted to the conditions of a totalitarian state than the theory of production and distribution of a given production put forth under conditions of free competition and a large degree of laissez-faire."[9]

"Laissez-faire" means let alone. If the aristocracy were to let the common people alone, it could not steal their wealth. You would be able to keep for yourself the product of your own labor.

As *New York Times* economic writer Leonard Silk recently commented, the Keynesian revolution "...could be called the Hitlerian economic revolution, since the policy was first put into effect in Nazi Germany in the nineteen-thirties."[10]

In the nations of black Africa, reports appear of leaders reaching political decisions by means of voodoo or witchcraft. We in our scientific, Western society feel smugly superior when we hear such stories. But in fact, in the realm of money, we are just as mystical as the practitioner of voodoo, and our heads of state make decisions which are just as irrational and superstitious as those of the nations of black Africa.

In the realm of economics there is a virtual unanimity with regard to the following propositions:	*Which might be restated by the witch doctor as:*
It is possible to get something for nothing.	*Nothing is real.*
Economic growth is greatly affected by what people think it will be. That is, if people think there will be prosperity, then there will be; if people think there will be blight, then that will occur.	*Appearance is reality.*

Thus the most important
element necessary for prosperity is confidence.
Value can be created by the   *Magic*
waving of a wand by the head
of the state (fiat money).
There is no excuse for these beliefs. They are rank superstition
out of the Middle Ages. The men who hold them are not scientists
and can not help us to deal with reality.

FOOTNOTES

[1] Max Farrand, *The Fathers of the Constitution* (New Haven, 1921), pp. 31-32.

[2] Evarts Boutell Greene, "The Revolutionary Generation 1763-1790," *A History of American Life*, eds. Schlessinger and Fox, IV (New York, 1943), p. 353.

[3] John Marshall, *The Life of Washington*, II, 1850 Edition, p. 99ff, as quoted by Charles A. Beard, *An Economic Interpretation of the Constitution of the United States* (New York, 1914), p. 297.

[4] *A History of American Life, op. cit.*, p. 353.

[5] David Ramsay, as quoted by Beard, *An Economic Interpretation of the Constitution, op. cit.*, p. 323.

[6] Beard, *op. cit.*, pp. 28-32.

[7] Jefferson, *Writings, op. cit.*, Answers to questions propounded by M. De Meusnier, Jan. 24, 1786.

[8] Keynes, *General Theory, op. cit.*, p. 15.

[9] John Maynard Keynes, German Edition of *General Theory of Employment, Interest and Money* (1936), as quoted by Henry Hazlitt, *The Failure of the "New Economics," An Analysis of the Keynesian Fallacies* (Princeton, 1967), p. 15.

[10] Leonard Silk, "Economics 1–The Summit," *The New York Times Magazine*, Sept. 22, 1974, p. 99.

CHAPTER VIII

What Really Goes On In The U.S. Economy

The corruption of Watergate has shown the American people some of the moral rot which infests our government. But Watergate is only the tip of the iceberg. The "failure" of successive presidents to end the steady rise in prices is not the result of incompetence or of the difficulty of the problem; without the active support of the Government the bankers could not expand their issues of paper money. Almost every president since FDR has played a game of betrayal and deceit. They have deliberately and consciously worked to further the interests of the aristocracy while maintaining a public image of being on the side of the people.

John F. Kennedy, our beloved martyred President, was a perfect example of the leader who maintains a liberal image but follows policies on behalf of the aristocracy. Kennedy's rather small budget deficits in the early 1960s aroused considerable conservative opposition. But the bankers knew how to get around that. Working with investment banker Henry Cabot Lodge in a bipartisan effort Kennedy, step by step, got us involved in a war in Vietnam.

The Pentagon Papers have revealed the deliberate deceit which occurred at that time. We now know that the United States did not enter the Vietnam War in response to North Vietnamese aggression as Lyndon Johnson claimed in July of 1965. In fact the U.S. had been engaged in attacks against North Vietnam ever since February 1964 via the covert operation 34A.

Liberal critics have soundly condemned the entire Vietnamese operation, but they miss one central point: Motive. Much has been written about false theories and immoral policies. But the Vietnam War was not a mistake, not for the men who led us into it. It was the war which gave us the large budget deficits and huge paper money expansion of the late 1960s and quieted conservative opposition to these unsound fiscal policies.

As the issues of paper money increased in the late '60s, we got a chance to see the invariable effects of basing a society on the principle of something for nothing.

Between 1965 and 1968 there was a wild period of emotionalism in the stock market. All kinds of gamblers and promoters appeared with wild get-rich-quick schemes. There was a growth in crime and drug use; there was massive social unrest; there was conscription for a foreign war; there was a diminution in individual freedom; the depreciation of the currency caused a decline in real wages; there was a growth of giant conglomerates. The typical effects of a paper money system were upon the nation.

As has been previously described, the paper money issues of the late '60s showed that the aristocracy had gone too far for its own good. The "New Breed" of wild-eyed promoters and "gunslingers" arose to give it a challenge, and it was necessary to hold back on the paper money for a while to destroy these new challengers.

The newly elected Nixon administration complied with the wishes of the corporate establishment. Even before the new administration had been sworn in, the Federal Reserve had moved to stop the issues of paper money. Total increase in the money supply in 1969 was only 2%.

Without the stimulus of paper money there was a sharp setback for big business. The stock market fell sharply. From 1970 to 1971 corporate profits dropped 10%. GNP turned down. By the middle of 1970 the big business interests were hurting badly. The

Penn Central railroad collapsed. At one point, Chrysler and several big airlines were just a few weeks away from bankruptcy. The New York Stock Exchange itself was teetering on the brink.

The New York Stock Exchange had established a fund to reimburse the customers of any member firm which went bankrupt. This was necessary for the Exchange because had any substantial number of customers lost their money through a brokerage house failure, then people would have deserted the market in droves. It is hard enough in the market with the risks one takes in stocks (where there is opportunity for profit) without having to take further risks on your brokerage house. Yet by mid-1970, this fund was empty. The head of the NYSE spent the summer of 1970 running around the country patching up failing brokerage houses and arranging mergers. Had one major brokerage house failed and the customers not been reimbursed, millions of people would have left the stock market. Their selling would have further depressed the price of stocks and thrown more brokerage houses into bankruptcy causing the exodus to accelerate. Only a few people in the country realized it, but in the weeks after the Penn Central failure, American capitalism was on the verge of a major disaster.

(A parenthetical remark: On March 26, 1970, by surveying the paper money situation for the preceeding year, I was able to predict a 10-15% drop in corporate profits (DJI) and up to 5% drop in industrial production for the year 1970.[1] Actual results: 4% drop in industrial production; 10½% drop of corporate profits in the DJI. There was no Keynesian economist whose predictions were anywhere near as good. Pierre Rinfret, one of the "top" Nixon economists had gone around the country in 1969 saying, "There ain't gonna be no recession." The Friedmanites were better. They at least knew that there would be a recession, but they completely underestimated its magnitude.)

But by mid-1970, the "New Breed" had been totally destroyed. When the Penn Central bankruptcy occurred, the establishment became alarmed. The declared intention of the Nixon administration had been to stop "inflation," and this had not been accomplished by mid-1970. But with the "New Breed" out of the way the road was clear for another round of paper money.

First, American business began to cry "cost push inflation."

What they meant by this was that labor was demanding higher wages, which was of course true. However, it was not true that these higher wage demands were the cause of higher prices. As we have seen, the wages of labor lagged sharply behind prices during the business boom of 1965-1969. This gave the workers additional bargaining power in enforcing their demands. So labor was indeed able to enforce higher wages in 1970, but this was not at the expense of higher prices. It was at the expense of lower profits. So far from boosting prices, a gain in real wages generally occurs as the depreciation starts to slow. This is what happened from 1969 to 1971 as the rate of increase in the consumer price index fell from 6% to 3½%.

The aristocracy's solution to this dilemma was to resume the issues of paper money and restrict the wages of labor through price and wage controls. In 1971 and 1972 the money supply advanced at a rate of 8% per year. Corporate profits surged ahead; wages, after rising as a result of the recession, began to fall back again.

Because people have accepted the banker myth that a depreciation of the currency is inflation, i.e., a rise in goods, they believe that this rise in goods can be prevented by imposing price ceilings on goods. This is the theory behind price controls. Make a law that the price of a good cannot rise.

But goods are not rising; instead it is money which is falling; so such laws do no good. If you freeze the price of a good in terms of a depreciating currency, then you are forcing its price to fall in real terms.

Consider what would happen if a law were passed which forced the price of potatoes to fall? At first it would only cause grumbling from the potato growers. Then, as the price fell by a larger amount, they would become seriously alarmed. At some point all of their profit would be gone, and they would be selling potatoes at a loss. Before this point was reached, clearly, they would curtail their production. The result would be a shortage of potatoes.

And this is the inevitable result of price and wage controls. When they are imposed at a time of a depreciating currency, they cause shortages. This leads to black markets. Shortages of meat, paper, wheat and, of course, oil, as well as many other less well known items which occurred in 1973, merely reestablish this truth.

When the Nixon administration imposed price and wage controls on the American economy in August of 1971, it knew that such controls do not work. At that time Herbert Stein of the Council of Economic Advisers said to Dr. Murray Rothbard, "Don't worry Murray; Dick knows they won't work."[2]

At least price and wage controls do not work in the manner represented to the public. They do not prevent the depreciation of the currency. But they do work in a completely different manner. They convince the public that steps are being taken to stop "inflation." They keep up the pretense that the government is a government of the people, responsive to the popular will.

The adoption of price and wage controls by the Nixon administration in 1971 was a cynical measure declaring to those who understand economics that Nixon had decided *for* the continued depreciation of the currency and was looking for a way to assuage the inevitable public protest. Price and wage controls, therefore, should not be regarded as an "anti-inflationary" measure. They should be regarded as just the opposite. Their purpose is not to stem the rise in prices, which the administration pretends is being caused by some strange, outside force. Their purpose is to fool the public so that the continued issues of paper money can go on and on.

The housewives who boycotted meat in March of 1973 wielded a great deal of political power. Their united weight can topple almost any politician. But their action in the meat boycott was foolish and futile. The condition which they were protesting (had they sense enough to know it) was the fact that the aristocracy had robbed them through the depreciation of the currency. They were poorer and they had to do without. To voluntarily give up some of the goods which they could not have anyway is not a solution.

The reason meat prices rose sharply in early 1973 was that there was less meat. There were fewer goods for the common person because these goods had been taken by the aristocracy (as per the big rise in corporate profits in 1972 and 1973, for example). The average American worker *had* to consume less in 1973 because there was less for him to consume. An organized refusal to consume (which is what a boycott is) is not defiance of this condition; it is subservience. A march on the regional Federal Reserve Banks would have been a more effective protest.

Nixon's imposition of controls was particularly cynical because he knew what causes prices to rise. As he said in his 1968 campaign for election: "When federal expenditures are enormously more than federal revenues, the politicians pursuing popularity through inflation turn to the Federal Reserve system and create money—literally out of thin air. To finance the Treasury, the Federal Reserve system has expanded the money supply at a breathtaking rate. During 1967, the money supply grew at 7 per cent, the fastest rate of growth in the entire period since World War II."[3] But as long as the people do not know, the Government will continue to follow policies which benefit the banks and corporate interests. The housewives' plea to the President to "do something" was based on the assumption that, however incompetent, the President was fundamentally trying to solve their problem. This is false. The President is the main agent by which they are robbed. The increase in the money supply of 8% per year over 1971-72 was the cause of their distress in 1973.

What these women need is some economic education. Were that same force which was applied to the meat boycott to be applied to a demand for ending paper money, the budding aristocracy in America would be smashed.

In 1973 we again entered a period of "restraint" in the money supply. However, this was restraint only by comparison with the wild years of 1971 and 1972. The growth in the money supply in 1973 was approximately 5%, a rate higher than that of all but the most expansionary years in American history.

This time the aristocracy did not wait for a major corporation to go bankrupt. When President Ford took office upon the Nixon resignation, his first order of business was to end this period of "restraint." For this purpose Ford called a major conference of the economic priesthood for the month of September 1974. There was much disagreement among these distinguished "authorities" on all of the various fine points of their craft, but there was one recommendation which was virtually unanimous: This was for an easing of credit by the Federal Reserve.

As readers of this book already know, the way the Federal Reserve eases credit is by supplying Federal Reserve bank notes to the private banks, which in turn create additional money in the process of making loans. "Easing of credit" is a euphemism for a further increase in the production of paper money. The September conference was ostensibly called to find a solution to the problem of rising prices. The "solution" agreed upon by the economic priesthood was to step up the rate of issues of paper money. By a unique coincidence, the Federal Reserve announced that it had adopted just this solution in late August, shortly before the conference met.

In early 1975 the Ford administration gave up even the pretext of trying to stop the depreciation and adopted a radical Keynesian program. The Federal Budget deficit for fiscal 1976 was projected at 60 billion dollars. Members of the priesthood called for the creation of record amounts of new money. As this book goes to press, it is a safe, if pessimistic, conclusion that during this cycle the banks will surpass even the eight per cent increase in paper money of 1972.

It does not require a great understanding to predict the destruction of America in the next few generations. It simply requires knowledge of two events—the abandonment of the domestic gold standard on March 6, 1933 and the abandonment of the international gold standard on August 15, 1971.

The abandonment of the domestic gold standard and the declaration of Federal Reserve notes as legal tender in 1933 paved the way for major issues of paper money, which have by this time caused a large depreciation of our currency along with its attendant evils; crime, social unrest, war, a decrease in freedom and a shift of wealth from the poor to the rich. But during the period prior to 1971, there was a restraint on the issues of paper money. For most of this time, foreigners had the right, denied to Americans, to demand that their Federal Reserve notes be redeemed for gold. This always served as a check on the issue of paper money because, via international trade, foreigners were acquiring American dollars, and if this money started to depreciate too rapidly, they would turn it in for gold. This threat of a foreign run on the central bank's gold stock served to restrain the Federal Reserve from excessive issues of paper money.

But on August 15, 1971, President Nixon refused to honor even this right. The U.S. currency is now unrestricted paper. And there is no bar to as many issues of paper money as the aristocracy finds expedient. If the period from 1933 to 1971 was a period of mild currency depreciation, then the period from 1971 on will be a period of rampant currency depreciation.

To one trained to see, the meaning of the actions of August 15, 1971, was clear. The meaning of the gold embargo was to remove the check on paper money represented by potential foreign claims on our gold. The meaning of price and wage controls was to serve as a sop to divert public attention and convince people that the President really wanted to stop the rise in prices. These were the two steps which were necessary to clear the way for unrestricted issues of paper money.

To one trained to see, it was obvious as of August 16, 1971, that the decision had been made for paper money. Unless this decision is reversed, it will lead to the destruction of the United States.

The effects of a currency depreciation are not taught in our schools. But they are a common occurrence throughout history. For example, the Civil War currency depreciation—the product of the legal tender laws of 1862 and the borrowing for the war—was described by Clarkson Nott Potter to the Supreme Court as follows:

> Who can deny that a whole community is being demoralized, as under such a system of paper money communities everywhere and at all times have been demoralized? Who can deny that men will do now what they would have shrunk from ten years ago, before this system existed? When the wicked prosper, other men make haste to do likewise. And now not from the cities only, but from every part, men seek the great marts to try their fortunes in the ventures of the hour, hoping to gather where they have not strewn. Gambling in stocks, with the dangerous combinations it invites, and the corruption which it encourages, has become general; so that it is deemed venial to artificially inflate or depress prices, to create fictitious values by forced scarcedness or undue

depression by combined attacks. And whatever danger may come to the public debt of this great country, will come, not from the unwillingness of the people to pay; not from their want of ability to pay but will come, if it should come at all, from the recklessness of a people carrying out their schemes upon the waves of an inflated currency, and from the demoralization which such speculation produces. How can it be expected that this people will make the sacrifices necessary to enable their government to keep its pledged faith, when it has not only failed to keep its own faith with its creditors, but has filled its coffers from the sale of licenses to men to wrong each other by short payments, and has made haste to ratify, by the decision of its supreme tribunal, the constitutionality and rightousness of such a course?[4]

This was 100 years ago, but how very like the present. Potter is talking about the likes of Jay Gould, Jim Fisk and Daniel Drew. But he could be talking about our own Allen Klein, Fred Mates or Bernard Cornfeld.

And we find the following description of England during the currency depreciation of the Napoleonic Wars:

Nature seemed to make common cause with war and bad finance. The winter of 1812 was extraordinarily severe, and the accidents by flood and fire were numerous. *Crimes began to multiply* in that accord between physical distress and moral decay so often noticed. *Wages were down at starvation point.* Spinners had 7s. 6d. per week in a time of high prices for the necessaries of life. The recent introduction of machinery and the extension of the factory system would have caused an inevitable period of pressure on hand workers. Now these causes fell in with others to enhance the distress. The artisans, in striking analogy with our own farmers at the present time, sought their foe in the nearest and most palpable shape in which the bad circumstances of the time pressed upon them. They attacked the machines, burned the factories, and *united in riotous disturbances.* The *corn laws were in full force,* and prevented the relief which might have come from other countries in time of scarcity, while *manufacturers were entangled in a mesh of restrictions,* more ruinous even than Napoleon's Decrees or the Orders in Council.[5]

Here again we see crime, a decline in real wages, civil unrest, war and restrictions on freedom. Throughout history we find the fate of nations attached to the soundness of their currency. The fall of the Western Roman Empire was accompanied by a depreciation of its currency while the Eastern Empire survived. The Ottoman Empire lasted for 800 years with sound money and collapsed half a century after starting its debasement. England, after the Napoleonic Wars, established the pound as a gold currency and attained her period of greatness through the 19th century. But when the attempt to return to the gold standard failed after WW I, England quickly became a second rate country.

The reason for this is that paper money is the principle of something for nothing, and a society founded on the principle of something for nothing can not survive. Money is used by everyone in our modern society, and when money is corrupted, a corruption enters the bloodstream of our social life. Those who prosper are no longer the Horatio Alger types who prospered in the 19th century and built the country by their own success. They are fly-by-night promoters and gamblers who construct jerry-built conglomerates and know more about public relations than about operations. The beaver has been put out, and in his place is the leech—the man who prospers by taking from others.

When the road to success in a society is by legalized robbery, then the men in that society fall to eating each other. "When the wicked prosper, other men make haste to do likewise." That is what we in America are doing now. The evil are eating up the good, and when they have finished with that, they will eat each other.

We have seen how paper money is a system of Robin Hood in reverse. It robs from the poor to give to the rich. And we have seen that one of the ways in which it does this is by robbing the creditor to give to the debtor.

During a period of currency depreciation, businessmen struggle to get into large debtor positions. But they find that banks will not lend very much to small companies. There is therefore a trend toward merger and conglomeration in a period of currency depreciation.

When we study the history of the 17th and 18th centuries—periods of paper money—we find business dominated by huge multi-national corporations, such as the Hudson Bay Trading Company and the East India Tea Company. In the 19th century—the period of the gold standard—we find business dominated by Jefferson's little man. But in the 20th century, in direct proportion as prices rise, we find the giant corporation and the conglomerate replacing the small businessman. IT&T has come to have almost the same status in the 20th century that the East India Tea Company had in the 18th. It has special relationships high in the government; it intervenes in the internal affairs of foreign countries. Contrast this with the age of the so-called Robber Barons; the fact of the matter is that by 1896, after 30 years of declining prices, most of the railroad system of the nation was in receivership.

To even the most casual observer it is apparent that conglomerates are highly inefficient forms of business organization. The chain of command from top to bottom is too long; incentive gets lost along the way; corporate deadwood accumulates; the heads of the corporation do not know enough about all of the aspects of the business to make intelligent decisions. The reason the conglomerate survives today is because it is head over heels in debt—more in debt than its individual divisions could be were they separate companies. As the currency depreciates, the conglomerate pays off its debts with cheaper dollars.

Because the currency depreciation lowers real wages and because it harms creditors, it leaves both employees and creditors with an income below what the free market would have given them. Both of these groups, therefore, have additional bargaining power which they can use to remedy their situation. It has been generally recognized that a constant rate of "inflation"—whatever the rate—would eventually be ironed out by the bargaining process so that all social injustices caused by the currency depreciation would be compensated. For example, if it were generally understood in a society that the currency would depreciate by 10% a year, then creditors could demand an additional 10% added to their rate of interest to compensate for the loss of the principal; workers could demand an additional 10% added to their increase in wages.

But in such a society, since creditors and workers were not

losing, the aristocracy could not gain. To keep its illicit profits the aristocracy must continually *increase* the rate of paper money expansion, thus increasing the rate of currency depreciation. For example, big business found that a 3½% currency depreciation in 1965 (up from 1% in the early '60s) was fine for profits. But a 3½% currency depreciation in 1971 (down from 6% in 1969) was very bad for profits. By 1971 workers were demanding higher wage increases, and creditors were demanding higher interest rates. The only way the aristocracy can continue its profits is by increasing the currency depreciation to a new higher rate (as they did in 1972).

Because of this, people who are retired will find prices rising faster and faster, beyond anyone's capacity to plan. At an 8% annual depreciation the value of money will drop in half in eight years. This means that at that rate a person who provides for a $10,000 annual retirement income at age 65 will have a $5,000 annual income by age 73 and a $2,500 annual income by age 81. Of course, since the rate of currency depreciation will not remain constant at 8% but will continually accelerate, the only way a man can avoid becoming a ward of the state is by an early death.

Furthermore, since both workers and creditors have additional bargaining power on the free market, the aristocracy finds economic freedom opposed to its interests. When its profits are under pressure, therefore, it will move to use its political power to restrict freedom in economic affairs. (The most recent clear example of this was, as noted, the imposition of price and wage controls in 1971 after corporate profits had fallen by 10% in the previous year.)

But of course freedom is not divisible. As the Communist states demonstrate, you cannot take away people's economic freedom without taking away their freedom in all other areas as well.

This is why the aristocracy is riding a tiger. The American people will not put up with depredations on their freedom. They will not put up with continually rising prices. They will protest and make things too hot for any political party which leads them in this direction.

There is only one way the American people can be led to accept such infringements on their freedom. This is as part of a war emergency. The chart in Chapter III of the value of the U.S. dollar shows a remarkable concurrence between currency depreciation and war. This is not an accident. Paper money and war naturally go together. They have done so ever since the Bank of England was founded as part of a war emergency. It requires no special insight on my part to predict that, unless moves are made in the direction of stopping paper money, the gold embargo of August 15, 1971 will lead to a major war. The aristocracy will have to involve the country in a war to divert the public hostility from itself—or more accurately from policies and politicians it supports—to a foreign enemy. It is a device as old as the centuries.

But the situation is not hopeless. The decision has been made for paper money, but that decision can be reversed. The people who suffer from paper money are by far the majority. All that is necessary is for them to demand an end to the depreciation of the currency.

People must be given the freedom to reject paper money. The legal tender enactments, which have no constitutional basis, must be repealed by the Congress or declared null and void by the courts. Now that it is again legal to own gold the people will then be able to choose whether they will accept paper money or gold money.

Since the vast majority of people lose under paper money, they are sure to choose gold. This will cause the collapse of the establishment which lives off the labor of others. Then the Federal Reserve System must be abolished, and the old practice of banks of issuing more paper than they have gold with which to redeem it must be classified as fraud and prohibited by law.

The present generation of Americans has been betrayed by its fathers. That generation inherited a free and prosperous country based on a sound currency where a man could succeed on his own ability. They have passed onto their children a corrupt system based on deceit and exploitation. But the sins of the fathers will be visited upon the children. It is the coming generation which will suffer these ills unless it acquires the *understanding* to rise up and demand an end to paper money.

This book began with a quotation from Isaiah, and throughout it, the point has been made that currency depreciation and its host of attendent evils are not new but have destroyed many cultures prior to our own. Things were no different in Isaiah's time. They did not have paper money, but the kings fashioned fiat money by mixing base metals with the silver.

The prophet reports:	*In other words:*
How is the faithful city	
become a harlot!	*Crime*
it was full of judgement;	
righteousness lodged in it;	
but now murderers.	
Thy silver is become dross,	*Fiat money*
thy wine mixed with water:	*Bad business practices*
Thy princes are rebellious, and	*Corruption in government*
companions of thieves:	
every one loveth gifts, and	*Feeding the rich*
followeth after rewards:	
they judge not the fatherless,	*By oppressing the poor*
neither doth the cause of	
the widow come unto	
them. (Isaiah i:21-23)	

That society did not listen; it became involved in war and suffered a terrible catastrophe. It is my earnest hope that this book will be successful in imparting sufficient understanding to the American people that a similar fate will not befall us.

FOOTNOTES

[1] Howard Katz, *The Speculator*, March 26, 1970.

[2] This incident was related by Professor Rothard in a speech delivered in early 1972.

[3] Richard Nixon, "A New Direction for America's Economy," *Campaign Pamphlet*, July 6, 1968.

[4] Clarkson Nott Potter, Supreme Court Reports, *Legal Tender Cases* 12 Wall 514.

[5] William G. Sumner, *A History of American Currency* (New York, Greenwood Press, 1968), pp. 281-82. My emphasis.

AFTER WORD

It will come as a strange thought to most people that they live in a society in which our respected leadership, our important figures of authority, our higher experts, are frauds who make use of their positions to exploit the very people who believe in them.

But it should not. Most human societies throughout history have been based on similar false authorities and pseudo-experts. The peasant of the Middle Ages looked up to and respected the priest, who told him it was God's will that he submit to injustice and tyranny. The Indian Medicine Man was regarded with awe by the tribesmen. It did not matter that his complicated rain dances did not bring rain.

For the reader who asks, *"What can I do? How can I oppose this evil?"* the answer is as follows: The aristocracy is a small group; together with all the interest groups which benefit from its policies it constitutes less than 5% of the population. 5% of the people cannot oppress the other 95% by force; they must do so by deception. When the majority understand the nature of the evil which is exploiting them, they will easily throw it off through the political process.

This is the key—understanding. It was to prevent such understanding from reaching the people that the medieval aristocracy surpressed freedom of speech. It is for the same reason that Communist and Fascist rulers suppress it today. But theirs are more blatant tyrannies. Our newly emerging American aristocracy has not yet won such power.

"What can I do to defeat the aristocracy?" The answer is: Spread the understanding of the nature of our paper money system. It was for this purpose that this book was written. Spread the ideas presented here. Talk to your friends and neighbors about them. Explain them to your fellow workers. Urge them to read this book.

Most people are afraid of economics. The priests of the new aristocracy have spent most of their time complicating the subject so that it is incomprehensible to the average person. Like the formulae of the African Witch Doctor, most economics today is composed of meaningless gibberish, the only purpose of which is to impress the layman who feels that because he cannot understand it, it must be very important.

But true economics is understandable and in accord with common sense. There is nothing in it which is beyond the average person. If this understanding can be brought to the majority of people, then the aristocracy will be destroyed, and we will again live in a free society. If it is not, then the currency depreciation and its chain of attendant evils will gradually envelop the world, and the predictions of Chapter I will become reality.

APPENDIX A

THE CALCULATION OF GROSS NATIONAL PRODUCT

In constructing a measure of the total wealth of the country, economists come up against a major difficulty. It is that the units in which wealth exists are incommensurable; i.e., they are quantities which cannot be added together. The wealth of an average American consists of things like; a car, a house, meat, potatoes, bread and butter, a beautiful painting over his mantle, a college education for his child, an operation for his mother, a record player, etc. Now how does one add these things together? Well, a start might be made by breaking the car down into its component parts; 2,000 pounds of steel, 50 pounds of lead, 25 pounds of rubber, 5 pounds of copper, 20 pounds of upholstery, etc. Here, at least, the quantities are commensurable, but one has the sinking feeling that adding them up really doesn't mean too much. For example, adding the above items we get 2,100 pounds. But is this really a measure of the man's wealth in the car? If someone were to take away his car and give him 2,200 pounds of steel, would he be wealthier? The answer is clearly no. But in that case he would have 2,200 pounds instead of 2,100.

The conclusion that must be drawn is that weight is not a measure of wealth. Further, when we came to add in the later items, how would we add 2,100 pounds of car to a three hour operation for one's mother? Pounds and hours are totally incommensurable and cannot be added in any way whatsoever.

To resolve this difficulty economists translate each item of wealth into money terms by virtue of its price; car = $2,500, house = $30,000, food for one year = $2,000, painting = $50, college education = $10,000, operation = $1,000, record player = $250. Now these money amounts can be added to give a total. And this is what Gross National Product is. It is the *money value* of all the wealth produced in the nation. But there is an assumption made in using not the item itself or its weight but *its price.* This is the assumption that the item is really worth the price paid for it. This assumption underlies all attempts to measure a nation's wealth.

Is this assumption true? Well, on its behalf we can say one thing. If the man bought the car of his own free choice, then it is *his* judgement that it is worth *at least* $2,500. Otherwise why would he have paid that much for it? This is a reasonable assumption. He is the one who is using the car, and he is the one who is paying for it. If he thinks it is worth $2,500 to him, who are we to quarrel?

But this is a minimum figure. The car might very well be worth $4,000 to him. He pays only $2,500 because that is all he has to pay. Thus these figures going into GNP do not represent actual wealth; they represent minimum wealth. With regard to these figures we can say that that portion of the wealth of the country measured by them is *at least* the given figure. If, for example, because of labor difficulties the auto companies had to raise the prices of their cars while their quality was deteriorating (not an impossible event in this day and age), then the price of the car might go up to $3,000, and its value to our friend go down to $3,500. Our friend would still buy the car (albeit with much grumbling), but now the contribution to GNP made by that car would go up (because the price was higher) while the value would go down. The GNP would be higher because of this, but the wealth of the nation would be lower!

(The above paradox accurately describes what has happened on the New York subway system. The price of a subway ride is higher, and threatening to go still higher. Yet the service has deteriorated. New Yorkers may reflect as they suffer the indignities of the 5:00 PM rush that their distress is computed as a gain in Gross National Product.)

Furthermore, the assumption that the item is worth the price paid for it, while true after a fashion for the private sector of the economy, does not hold at all for the public sector. For example, a bridge may cost $10 million to build, but what is the value of that bridge to the motorists who use it? There is clearly some value—the time, gasoline and wear and tear saved by being able to go via the shorter route made possible by the bridge. But will these savings by all the motorists using the bridge over all the years of its life equal $10 million? There is simply no way of knowing. They may total $1 million, or they may total $20 million. Faced with a situation like this, economists simply throw up their hands and count the value of the bridge as equal to its cost. This, of course, is grossly in error and is done merely to get some kind of numerical value which can be added in to GNP. You or I could give them a number which would have as much meaning.

This use of cost to represent value has the following effect. If the contractor is honest and competent and builds the bridge for the scheduled $10 million, then the bridge counts as $10 million in GNP. But if he is dishonest and/or incompetent and requires $30 million to build the bridge, then it counts as $30 million in GNP. So in the public sector the greater the waste the greater the gain in GNP.

An example of this was the development of the F-111 fighter plane. As originally conceived by the Pentagon, it was to have swing wings so that the same plane could be used by both the Army and the Navy. Cost was to be $3.4 million/plane. If the job had been done according to specification, this would have been the addition to GNP from this source. But there were major cost overruns so that by 1967 the cost had risen to $9.5 million/plane.[1] And the engineering failures were so great that the plane was never made adaptable for the Navy. Because of this waste and incompetence the nation saw a greater addition to GNP from this source and a poorer quality product than if the original contracts had been met.

This of course brings up the whole question of whether military expenditures ought to be counted as part of GNP. The purpose of military expenditures is to provide for the defense of the nation. But if the President could negotiate a valid, enforceable treaty with the Communists which could guarantee our security, would not this treaty be as beneficial to the defense of the nation as all our armaments? Or if revolutions were to occur in the Communist world so that true republican forms of government arose in those areas and the new leaders established free elections and freedom of speech and unilaterally disarmed, would not this series of events be *more* beneficial to the security of the nation than all the money we spend on armaments each year? If such a treaty or such revolutions were to occur, the tremendous amount of labor and materials we spend on defense could be shifted over to produce things for people's use. Vast numbers of our citizenry would be better off because that portion of their tax money which now goes for bombs, tanks, and guns would go for products which truly improved their lot in the world.

Yet if such a change occurred, the benefit gained would not show up in GNP. The addition to GNP from goods to benefit people would counterbalance the decrease in GNP from the lower rate of defense spending. Peace treaties have no price and hence can not be counted in GNP.

Conversely, when a country goes to war, its real wealth goes down. People are poorer. On the one hand the public has been told that WW II pulled the country out of the Depression; on the other hand we are reminded of all the hardships of war. If an individual family finds that it is in a condition where the mother must work and yet there is not enough milk for the children, that family is regarded as poor. Yet that was the state of the nation in WW II. (There was a massive movement of women into the labor force; at the same time there were shortages of many items, including butter and milk.) Yet the economic indicators showed the country enjoying great prosperity during WW II—this at a time when the country was suffering a great loss in wealth. How then could these indicators accurately (or even approximately) measure wealth?

FOOTNOTES

[1] Robert Bleiberg, "Moment of Truth: It's Time the Nation Cut Its Losses on the TFX," *Barron's* Sept. 18, 1967, p. 1.

APPENDIX B

THE ROBBER BARONS VS THE MODERN BUSINESSMAN

It is one of the great myths of our age that the 19th century period of laissez-faire in the American economy was a time in which ruthless, unscrupulous businessmen exploited both their workers and consumers; and correspondingly, that the modern era is a period in which enlightened businessmen subordinate profits to their social responsibilities.

This myth is part of the fraud perpetrated by Keynesian and Marxist intellectuals to lay the basis for the exploitation of the poor by means of the depreciation of the currency and to pose as liberals and progressives while doing so. In fact the opposite is true. The 19th century was a period of great prosperity for the common man, and our own age is a time when the poor are exploited for the sake of the rich.

Let us consider two periods: A 30 year period of currency appreciation in the 19th century (chosen because it is the longest period of currency appreciation in American history) and a corresponding period of currency depreciation in our own age.

The charts in Illustration 6 make the point quite clearly. In the period of currency appreciation workers did better; in the period of currency depreciation capitalists did better. In the late 19th century, the railroad industry was a young, growth industry (like automobiles in the '20s or office equipment in the 1960s). Yet rail stocks, for all the supposed machinations of the "Robber Barons," could only muster a 68% real growth from 1871 (earliest year figures are available) to 1896. In the modern era the railroad industry is an old, sick industry, sluggish in its growth and outpaced by almost every other group. Yet due to the depreciation of the currency, rail stocks grew by 250% in real terms during this period.

Corresponding figures for workers show the same story. While our modern workers, deceived by politicians who pretend to be their friends, gained less than 50% in real terms in a period of currency depreciation, the 19th century workers, supposedly under the thumb of the Robber Barons, showed a real gain of 90%.

ILLUSTRATION 6A

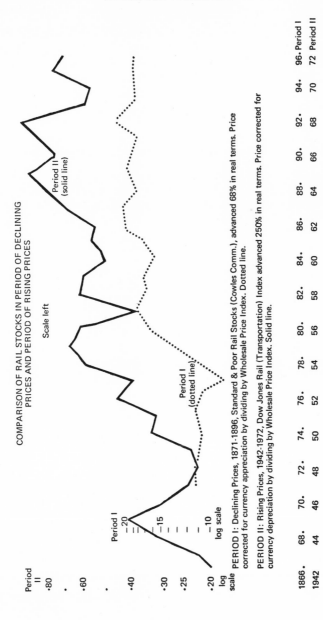

COMPARISON OF RAIL STOCKS IN PERIOD OF DECLINING
PRICES AND PERIOD OF RISING PRICES

PERIOD I: Declining Prices, 1871-1896, Standard & Poor Rail Stocks (Cowles Comm.), advanced 68% in real terms. Price corrected for currency appreciation by dividing by Wholesale Price Index. Dotted line.

PERIOD II: Rising Prices, 1942-1972, Dow Jones Rail (Transportation) Index advanced 250% in real terms. Price corrected for currency depreciation by dividing by Wholesale Price Index. Solid line.

ILLUSTRATION 6B

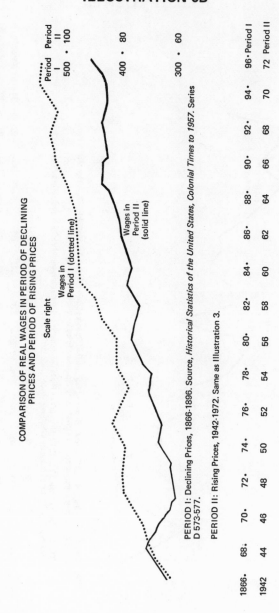

COMPARISON OF REAL WAGES IN PERIOD OF DECLINING PRICES AND PERIOD OF RISING PRICES

Scale right

Wages in Period I (dotted line)

Wages in Period II (solid line)

PERIOD I: Declining Prices, 1866-1896. Source, *Historical Statistics of the United States, Colonial Times to 1957.* Series D 573-577.

PERIOD II: Rising Prices, 1942-1972. Same as Illustration 3.

INDEX